LOVE, *j*ACK

LOVE, JACK

by

GUNILLA VON POST

~

with

CARL JOHNES

Crown Publishers, Inc.

NEW YORK

Photograph on title page copyright © Yale Joel, *Life* Magazine © Time Inc.
Wedding photograph courtesy AP/Wide World Photos.

Published by Crown Publishers, Inc., 201 East 50th Street, New York, New
York 10022. Member of the Crown Publishing Group.

Random House, Inc. New York, Toronto, London, Sydney, Auckland
http://www.randomhouse.com/

CROWN and colophon are trademarks of Crown Publishers, Inc.
Printed in the United States of America
Design by Lynne Amft
Library of Congress Cataloging-in-Publication Data

von Post, Gunilla
    Love, Jack / by Gunilla von Post with Carl Johnes.
        p. cm.
    1. Kennedy, John F. (John Fitzgerald), 1917–1963—Friends
and associates.   2. von Post, Gunilla, 1932–   .   3. Presidents—
United States—Biography.   I. Johnes, Carl.   II. Title.
E842.1V66   1997
973.922'092—dc21
[B]   97-15361
                                                              CIP

ISBN 0-609-60095-8
10   9   8   7   6   5   4   3   2   1
First Edition

To the memory of my beloved sister, Ewa.

CONTENTS

FOREWORD

I first met Gunilla von Post a couple of years ago in New York, while she was en route from Switzerland to Florida. I'd been put in touch with her through an actress friend who knows at least two hundred unusual people on every continent, and had said, "She's Swedish. She has an interesting story to tell. Why don't you talk to her?" On a brisk November evening, I joined Gunilla and her son for dinner at a bustling bistro on Manhattan's East Side. Our conversation that night was indeed interesting, providing tantalizing evidence of a great true love story, as yet untold.

Our relationship grew slowly, via telephone calls, letters, and meetings. Finally, in the fall of 1995, I flew to Palm Beach for ten days and Gunilla and I began to collaborate. Our first task was piecing together the handwritten love letters John F. Kennedy had sent her from 1954 through the summer of 1956—letters she had saved for forty years. As she recalled details of their courtship, their bittersweet romance, and their unexpected but heart-stirring reunion in 1958, a portrait of Mr. Kennedy emerged that was new—that of a tender, affectionate young man, very different from the coolly ambitious and philandering JFK of the tabloids.

As I heard Gunilla's story, I realized that despite the millions of words already written about him, this century's most famous American has remained a figure glimpsed through a prism as diffused as any view of history. The vision Gunilla was sharing with me showed facets of our thirty-fifth president that hadn't been revealed until now.

Our days and nights of talk, writing, and dinners opened up names, dates, places, and feelings that Gunilla thought were long forgotten. Still, these were therapeutic hours filled with more laughter than pain.

Throughout, we tried as much as possible to capture Gunilla's spirit. More important, we sought to transmit a memorably emotional experience onto the page.

What you are about to read is the result of this effort, a personal, unique reminiscence of John F. Kennedy, related in the ingenuous voice of the woman he not only loved but also wished to marry—his most secret, and perhaps truest, young love.

Besides revealing a sensitive, vulnerable JFK captured through her own intimate lens, Gunilla's memoir is the story of a haunting romance, a "brief, shining moment"—before Camelot, before an assassin's bullets *shattered the hopes of the country and a generation of Americans—a moment in time that Gunilla von Post is at last ready to share with the world.*

—Carl Johnes
NEW YORK, 1997

LOVE, JACK

PALM BEACH: 1994

I awakened later than usual on the morning of May 20, in my apartment on Coconut Row. While making coffee, I glanced through the window but couldn't quite make out the weather. I took my cup outside onto the little terrace just off my dining room and looked up. There were still some gray clouds hiding the sun.

It was Friday, and a busy weekend lay ahead. I was due to fly to New York on Saturday for a quick visit with my son, Wisner, then take a flight over the Atlantic to my small but cozy flat in the Swiss village of Villars-sur-Ollon. There, up in the Alps, I would be able to see my firstborn, Andrea, and her six-year-old boy, Janni, my adorable grandchild, then head on to Portugal to stay with my younger daughter, Rosina, her husband, and their children, Eduardo, Isabel, and Ricardo.

But today I would relax. My only plans were to meet a few friends at the beach club for lunch and a swim. Better check to see if the sun was going to make an appearance. I found the television remote tucked among the pillows and magazines on a chair, and clicked it on. I pressed MUTE, as is my habit—the world being quite noisy enough—and watched the screen brighten.

Instead of the usual morning quiz shows and talk programs, I saw a painfully serious-looking newscaster talking from behind his desk. The next on-screen image was the face of a very famous woman, and underneath her was a subtitle:

JACQUELINE KENNEDY ONASSIS
1929-1994

I clicked the sound back on as John F. Kennedy, Jr., appeared in front of his mother's Fifth Avenue apartment house. He said she had died "in her own way . . . And we all feel lucky for that."

Stunned as I was, I placed my cup slowly down on the coffee table and sat just as slowly and carefully on my sofa, trying to compose myself and hoping that the pounding within my chest would cease. But this was a watershed moment; for me, the past had collected itself into a complete picture, one I could see whole now.

I was aware that Jacqueline had been ill, of course, but the reality of this news was still a shock. The announcer's voice droned on. I turned off the TV. I wasn't listening to him. I was listening to my own thoughts.

I had heard about moments when a lifetime flashes before one's eyes. Now several lifetimes ran quickly by:

mine, and Jacqueline's, and that of a third person who had made an indelible imprint upon both of us.

I had always felt a sisterhood with Jackie. We had both lost an infant son. We had both been widowed, in the cruelest possible way.

I had watched her as she raised John Jr. and Caroline. Her dignity and public demeanor had inspired me to be a good mother to my fatherless children, too. We were of the same generation, born only three years apart, and we each had enjoyed the comforts of a privileged upbringing—mine as the offspring of an old Swedish/German family whose ancestors could be traced back to ancient Scandinavian nobility, and Jacqueline, a daughter of French nobility.

But we had suffered agonizing tragedies, the two of us. And we had survived. And once, we had both loved the same man.

I picked up my coffee and drank a few sips. It was tepid by now, but I didn't mind. My memory was reaching back, far back, to something important that began over four decades earlier.

Could I ever tell anybody my story? I certainly never would have while Jacqueline was alive. But would her children understand? Would mine? What would people think of me? Did I want to let the world know about a moment in time that was precious, private—and magical?

I grabbed the phone and dialed. "Hello, dear. It's Gunilla. I'm going to be late for lunch. No, no, nothing's wrong. Just—start without me. I'll be there in a while."

I left the apartment house and drove across Brazilian Avenue to South Ocean Boulevard. I wanted to walk by the sea, to hear the waves, to feel the breeze and the salty spray against my skin. The ocean has always been a healing power for me.

Stopping at one of the railings overlooking the water, I looked up. I thought back to another day, on another beach, forty years in the past. I reached for my dark glasses as the clouds burned off.

My heart was filled with emotion; the memories came back to me, as bright and clear as the sky had become—as blue now as it was on the afternoon we met. The waves had a similar soft and steady splash. And above was the same sun that had shone down upon me—and upon him—an ocean away, and a lifetime ago.

CÔTE D'AZUR: 1953

Anne Marie and I raced each other out of the Mediterranean Sea and up across the beach, laughing all the way. Afterward, we lay on the sand, luxuriating in the warmth of a sun that shone much less often in our native Sweden.

I was twenty-one years old, it was August, and I was on the Riviera. My friend Anne Marie Linder and I had been sent there from Stockholm by our families for the month. We were lodged at La Bourgade, a small, charming, stone-and-wood-beam nineteenth-century villa rented from the Swedish/Finnish Baronness Wrede, nestled up in the hills of Haut-de-Cagnes, about twelve miles straight north of Cap d'Antibes. Officially, we were there to improve our French.

We spoke as much French as we could to the local people, but we also had several good Swedish friends with whom we could talk. We traveled around the area in taxis and the cars of our friends. My distant cousin Sverker Åström, who later was at the United Nations in New York, and served as our ambassador to Paris, often swam with Anne Marie and me at the stony little beach in Cagnes, below La Bourgade.

But on this particular day, Anne Marie and I had managed to make it to the famous *plage* at Cannes alone. It was an exciting place to be, full of glamorous people and big hotels.

The sun was no longer beating down from directly above, but was beginning to move west. "We'd better go," I said to Anne Marie. Our suits weren't quite dry, and my blond hair was still a little tangled and salty, but I put on my yellow sundress and got ready to leave.

There had been a nationwide postal strike, and our allowances from home hadn't arrived for three weeks. We were not only running out of cash, but for the last week we'd been living on only bread, cheese, and red wine.

"How will we get home?" Anne Marie asked.

I thought fast. We ran up the stairs to La Croisette, the main thoroughfare of Cannes, and started walking slowly. Looking around at the traffic, I stuck my thumb in the air.

A dark blue British sedan, heading toward Nice, slowed down and then stopped fifty yards away from the Hotel Carlton. The driver wore a casual resort out-fit, and he was good-looking, tanned, and strongly built, with brown-green eyes. He appeared to be some-where in his early forties, and he was polite, even courtly—a gentleman, and not at all dangerous. We ac-cepted his offer of a ride.

His name was Gavin Welby, and we learned that he was an English businessman. After scolding us slightly for hitchhiking, he asked where we were staying, and then invited us to join him for dinner at Le Château, "which is quite near your house, it's very romantic, and the food is good. I think you'll enjoy it."

We accepted his offer with great pleasure. A few minutes later I was sitting back, looking out at the boats and ships floating in the water, when suddenly Mr. Welby pulled to a stop at the Port of Antibes. "Jack!" he called out. "What the hell are you doing here?"

A tall, slender young man with tousled light auburn hair walked by. He had a casual look about him, mostly because of his offhand style of dress. His tan washed pants were clean but unpressed, as if he'd pulled them right off the clothesline and put them on. His shirt was similarly casual—faded, short-sleeved, and even more wrinkled than my sundress. But his eyes were intensely blue, sparkling with joy, as if there were stars in them. And he had a smile that lit up his entire face. He turned and, recognizing Gavin, immediately walked over toward our car.

"Gavin!" he said, shaking his head with relief. "Am I glad to see you! I'm being chased by this Italian contessa on a Vespa, and I don't know how to get rid of her. She's driving me crazy." He sounded American, with a fascinating accent I'd never heard before. But whatever the accent was, his sensuous voice was strong and dynamic.

The tall young man glanced at us, but Welby didn't make any introductions. The young man's expression was curious. "What are you up to, Gavin?" he asked.

"We're going to have dinner at Le Château in Haut-de-Cagnes. Why don't you join us?"

He looked at me with those piercing, tender blue eyes. "I'll see what I can do," he said, and he was off into the crowds again.

Gavin Welby told us he was John Kennedy, a United States senator from Massachusetts. That meant nothing to me, and I forgot the name before we arrived at our house to change for dinner. But I couldn't forget those eyes, and I hoped with an intensity that surprised me that I would see him again that evening.

～

Le Château was indeed romantic and beautiful. It was housed in an old villa, much larger than La Bourgade, with high ceilings and views of the rolling hills and valleys of Cagnes. We arrived just as the sun was setting, its glow enhancing the rose-pink table settings. The room was already crowded with guests and busy waiters, befitting a chic restaurant in high season.

As Anne Marie and I walked into the dining room in our simple but elegant dresses, I felt an exciting rush of joy. There was Jack—the tall American from Antibes—already sitting in a corner banquette. I was tremendously relieved, because I had feared he might not show up. But there he was—wearing a light gray suit and an open white shirt, looking nervous in a boyish, sheepish way. I was surprised at myself; the sight of him made me so happy.

"Hello!" Jack said right away to all three of us. He stood and looked straight into my eyes. Something happened at that moment. It was as if part of Jack's soul leapt directly into mine. He was immediately attentive to me.

He held out his hand to me. "Jack Kennedy," he said.

"Gunilla von Post," I responded.

Gavin took Anne Marie's hand and, after leading her into the corner banquette seat, slid in next to her. Jack did the same, so that he and I were also side by side. When we were settled, I turned to him and said, "I'm sorry, I didn't hear your name."

"Kennedy! John Kennedy!" he repeated, much louder, but with more amusement than impatience.

In playful retaliation, he asked me how I spelled my name, and then he said, "Well, it's a funny name. It sounds like Gorilla, and you are so tiny and delicate and pretty, I think I'll call you that!" And so he did. I was often "Gorilla" from then on.

I had met a few Americans, but never one like this. The Americans I'd met before certainly had the same kind of energy and curiosity as John Kennedy, but nothing approaching his ease. He was direct, open, and comfortable with himself. He was *right there* when you looked at him. I felt as though we had known each other for a long time.

I asked him, "Whatever happened to your friend today? The Italian contessa?"

With a youthful smile and downcast eyes, he replied, "I don't know. I don't care, actually. I'm here with you now."

For the rest of that evening, everyone else disappeared. I know we spoke occasionally to Anne Marie and Gavin, but I don't remember what little we said. Jack and I seemed to talk only to each other. With his penetrating gaze, and the riveting intensity of his deep blue eyes, we couldn't take our eyes off each other.

Moving closer to me, Jack leaned into my ear to speak, rather than raising his voice over the noise of the restaurant. "Is this your first time in France?" he asked.

"No. A few years ago I was sent by Baron Jan de Geer, the head of the Red Cross in Sweden, to work at a hospital for orphans outside Marseilles, but I got sick and had to go home early," I said. "My health is a bit fragile, but I have a strong will!" I surprised myself by saying this. Why was I able to speak so openly to a man I barely knew? It was because Jack made everything seem so easy.

He listened enthusiastically, and I found myself talking about everything. When he asked questions, he really seemed interested in the answers.

We discussed travel much of the time. Jack had been everywhere. My parents knew that travel was the best education, so just after my sixteenth birthday I'd been sent off to stay with a family in Lausanne, and later to Scotland as a guest at Seggieden, the castle near Perth presided over by the tall and engaging Jimmy Drummond-Hay and his wife, Lady Margaret Douglas-Hamilton.

"Lady Margaret was famous for her stables," I told him. "I rode the ponies there. I jumped. I don't know the English for that." I ate a small piece of bread with my *soupe au pistou*.

Jack loved to watch me, a small woman, eat with such gusto. "So, did you go home after that?" he asked.

"Well, no. In a way, yes. I went to Douglas Castle, on the English/Scottish border, and stayed with the old Earl of Home and Lady Home. It's pronounced 'hume' but spelled like 'home.'"

Jack nodded. "I know. I've met their son William. He's a writer. And his brother Alex is in politics."

"Yes." Alex Douglas-Home was indeed in politics, and ten years later would become Britain's prime minister. "And the third brother, Henry, and their sister, Bridget."

Our main courses arrived. We had both ordered *sole meuniere,* a specialty of the house.

I caught Jack looking at me. The emotions running between us were very deep. He finally looked down and started his fish.

"Good?" I asked.

His eyes rested on me again. "Delicious," he said. I was excited just to be near him. He was such a powerful, magnetic man, it was hard to deny my growing attraction to him.

When he asked me how Anne Marie and I had come to know Gavin, my shyness returned. I told him the story of our hitchhiking.

"Well, well. And how did you manage that?" he asked.

I held up my hand and crooked my thumb. "Like this," I said. Unlike the stern disapproval I might have suffered from my Nordic aunts and uncles, Jack thought it was hilarious, and complimented me on my enterprise. He leaned over and whispered in my ear,

"And that's not really Gavin's style. He looks like a playboy, but he's conservative underneath."

"I think so, too," I whispered back. "He gave us a lecture. He said two nice girls like us could get into terrible trouble doing such a thing. So I told him about our desperate situation. He was so kind, I almost curtsied." The reason I didn't was because, three years earlier, I'd been presented to Princess Sibylla at the Court of Sweden, and as I lowered myself to curtsy, my knee gave out such a loud *crack!* that I thought it echoed throughout the courtroom. I'd turned red. Princess Sibylla looked down at me and smiled. "There, there, my dear," she'd said in her broken Swedish, "it wasn't so bad, was it?" But it was bad. And it cured me of the curtsy.

The light outside had nearly faded, and it seemed as though the chandeliers shone more brightly now. Jack couldn't stop showing affection for me, and I couldn't stop smiling at him. He took my hand, poured more wine, and looked directly into my eyes. He had great enthusiasm, as though everything in life were possible.

I started to feel strongly that underneath the light give-and-take of our conversation, something deeper and more intimate was happening. Jack talked about the Kennedy "compound" on the seashore, and told me about his family—his mother, Rose; his father, Joe;

and Joe Jr., who was killed in the war; and his two other brothers, Bobby and Teddy. I admitted to him that I'd always been a little intimidated by my younger sister, Ewa, who was so vivacious and clever, and he offered that living in the lingering shadow cast by his dead brother was a problem, too. Jack was desperate to please his father, much as I wanted to please my pappa, who was called "Olle," and my mother, Brita, both of whom had very high standards and rules of behavior that I was never sure I could fulfill. I started to understand that this boyish-looking man was carrying a heavy load on his shoulders.

Several of my friends had recently become interested in astrology and the signs of the zodiac. Even though some people made fun of it, I was told it was an ancient science, and it was one that fascinated me. I asked Jack his birth date.

"I was born on May 29, at three o'clock in the afternoon, 1917. And you?"

"Me? July 10, 1932. On the hottest day of the year. No air-conditioning, either. My poor mother!"

Jack smiled. "July 10. That's my sister Eunice's birthday, too. She just got married this past May."

I thought it was interesting that he'd not mentioned any sisters before this. Only brothers. I didn't know until much later that his parents had actually had nine children. But I didn't pry. I did wonder, though, since

Jack was a Gemini and I'd always heard that Geminis comprised two distinct personalities, which personality I was witnessing. Also, if his sister and I were Cancerians with exactly the same birth date, was there any kind of mystical compatibility between him and me? I put it this way:

"Do you like your sister Eunice?"

"I love Eunice," he said.

"Do you believe in destiny? In fate?" I asked.

He smiled in an offhand way, "Oh, I think my destiny is what my father wants it to be."

As if to change the subject, he reached up and gently pushed a strand of hair from my eyes, and I was grateful for the candlelight, because I blushed. When I was a baby, my father had nicknamed me Napoleona because of the little Napoleonic curl that kept flopping down onto the middle of my forehead. Pappa got into the habit of smiling down at me and brushing that wisp of hair aside. I knew as a child that it was a sign of affection, and I knew as a young woman feeling the first stirrings of love that Jack's simple gesture was the same thing.

After dinner, we all went over to Jimmy's Bar across the way. Jimmy's was actually a popular nightclub, quite elegant, with an orchestra and an outdoor dance floor. The band was playing when we got there, and Jack asked me to dance with him.

As he took me into his arms, I felt his body stiffen. He closed his eyes and seemed to concentrate on breathing evenly.

"We don't have to dance, Jack," I suggested.

He smiled and seemed to will away his pain. "Oh, yes we do!" he said. He held on and turned me around slowly. I was witnessing his back problems, the chronic condition he would endure throughout his life, something you would never suspect from his effervescent personality. But he didn't want me to notice. It was as if by holding me closer with each song the musicians played, the pain moved farther away.

He led us outside. Now we were under the stars, which I felt I could reach up and touch. The mimosa-like fragrance, typical of the Côte d'Azur, filled the air. The orchestra began a haunting melody that switched from minor into beautiful major chords in the middle. In a half-whispered light baritone, Jack began to sing, slightly but charmingly off-key,

"I love Paris in the springtime . . ."

He held me tighter than ever and whispered in my ear, "Do you love Paris?"

I said, "I haven't been there, but I've thought of going. My French is getting better. My English will improve."

I closed my eyes and smiled as Jack's arms enfolded me, allowing myself to dream of a wonderful life with this charismatic American. He said, "I feel as though I'm dancing with one of the most exciting, enchanting women in the world, and I'm very happy."

At two o'clock in the morning we were still dancing, and I felt I could go on forever, but Jack suggested that the four of us drive down to Eden Roc at Cap d'Antibes, where his family often stayed.

I know that Gavin and Anne Marie came along with us, but again, I have no recollection of what they did or where they were. When we arrived at Eden Roc, Jack and I sat on the edge of the cliff, and for the first time that night we were quiet together. The light wind lifted my hair, the Mediterranean splashed against the rocks below, and the stars glowed in the sky. Jack sat next to me, so close. It was as if the two of us were one in the world.

He turned and kissed me tenderly, and my breath was taken away. The brightness of the moon and stars made his eyes appear bluer than the sea beneath us. He broke the silence by saying softly, "I fell in love with you tonight."

I opened my mouth but couldn't speak. I looked away, down toward the sea.

"It's only happened to me once before," he said. "Five years ago, I fell in love with Grace Kelly the moment I saw her. The same thing has just happened now."

I shivered in the warm breeze.

Jack stopped looking at me and fixed his gaze somewhere far beyond the sea's horizon. "I have to tell you something," he said. He reached up and rubbed his cheek nervously. Both his hand and his voice were shaking. He looked and sounded stricken.

"I'm going back to the United States next week to get married," he said.

My shiver turned to a chill. I pulled my silk shawl tightly around my shoulders.

"If I had met you one week before," Jack continued, "I would have canceled the whole thing."

I glanced at him. His expression was one I hadn't seen before then that night. He looked defeated and sad. There were no words to describe the emotional tension in the air.

I was close to tears, but I admired him for his honesty. He could have just left that part out. I rose up first from the rock and said, "Well, that's that." I didn't ask who she was, or why he was marrying somebody he didn't seem to love. We walked slowly back to his car, and he drove me home.

We paused at the front door of the house at Haut-de-Cagnes. The entry was up a short flight of curved stone steps, which were shrouded in greenery, like a leafy cocoon. The bushes were dense, but you could still see the Mediterranean through them. The moon was still bright. It shimmered on the water far below, and it dappled Jack's face in the semidarkness. Leaning over me, with his hands resting lightly on my shoulders, he asked, "May I come in for a nightcap?"

"No, my dear Jack," I said.

He asked again, this time more insistently. "Gunilla, I've had such a wonderful evening. Can I stay a little longer?"

"But you are going away to get married," I said. "And I only want to wish you good luck, and that everything works out for you."

He didn't protest. His eyes said he understood. He gave me another long, deeply passionate kiss and left.

I closed the door and waited. I pulled aside the window curtain and looked out, then let it fall back, listening as he started his car. The sound of the engine finally disappeared into the night.

Then I cried.

~

I was out of my mind with a sense of loss. I missed him terribly, because I knew we could have been happy together. But then in the first week of September I had a sore throat, followed by a severe fever. By the end of the week, I was sent to the hospital and diagnosed with typhoid, which might have come from the water or the food in southern France, no one could tell. Penicillin shots at the hospital and then recuperation at La Californie in Cannes lowered the fever, but I remained very weak.

I saw the wedding pictures in magazines that September. The wedding party was impressive, with all the women in flowing white dresses, holding bunches of flowers. Jack's brother Bobby was best man, and the bride's sister, Lee, was matron of honor. Jacqueline Bouvier was very attractive and elegant, but she and I were so different, at least physically. I stared at her face and couldn't understand why Jack had said he loved me and yet was marrying a woman so dark, while I was so fair.

I also thought, That could have been me, and then scolded myself for thinking it. It was just a kiss. It's over, Gunilla, it's the end. You can't keep crying over an impossible dream. Now just get on with your life.

I stayed in Paris for a week, trying to recover, and then flew back to Stockholm at the end of the month. I was booked into tourist class for the flight, but my second cousin Claes Braunerhjelm happened to be up in first class and announced to the stewardess, "My cousin has typhoid fever, and she has to come sit with me." I did, and the entire first class got up and ran to the back of the plane!

I had another stay in the hospital upon my return to Sweden; my heart muscle inflammation made me weak for a long time. I began to worry that I might never have a normal life, that I might not be able to have children, but my physician, Dr. Börje Ejrup, assured me that with plenty of rest, good food, time, and patience, I would be completely well again.

Slowly, I did start to get better and get on with my life. It was a good life, too, after the fever was gone. There were parties, and a few beaus, but Jack had changed me. Now dating and boyfriends took on a different quality. I'd come close to the real thing with Jack, and other men paled beside him.

Even in the mid-1950s, Swedish people of our class maintained a style of living that was straight out of the nineteenth century. As a young girl, I remember very few excursions into public society. Traditionally, social life was confined to private homes. You received an invitation from the parents of friends or schoolmates, asking you to a *the dansant* (they later were really "wine dansants"), usually on a Sunday afternoon, all rather formal. I went to an all-girls' school, and the boys went to all-boys' schools, so a mingling of the sexes had to be carefully arranged. There would be food, and perhaps a piano player, and then the carpets were rolled back and everyone danced—in suits and sophisticated dresses. This was, for all practical purposes, the only way to meet boys up until the age of eighteen or so.

I met a few, one being a nice German boy, Wolf-Manfred von Richthofen, the nephew of the legendary fighter pilot "the Red Baron." He boasted that his father actually shot down more planes than his more famous uncle. But this imprimatur did not prompt me to fall in love.

Several months after I turned eighteen, there had been an admirer named Berth von Kantzow. He was Swedish and Austrian, and lived in Brazil. He came from an old family, and his father was a very good friend of my parents. He asked for my hand in marriage. I liked him a lot, but I was not quite nineteen. My maternal grandmother, Karin Elmér, who was as different from my mother as a cool glass of lemonade is from a glass of schnapps, later had her own opinion about Berth. Grandmother Karin wrote poetry and was considered eccentric. I was crazy about her. She and my grandfather had a house on the west coast, and Berth joined us for a party there to celebrate my nineteenth birthday. When he was offered a glass of champagne, he said, "Oh no, thank you. May I have a soft drink?" and my grandmother whispered to me quickly, "No, no, Gunilla, he's very nice, but he's *not* the man for you."

Now I began to wonder if I would ever meet "the man for me." Certainly none of them had affected me the way Jack had.

But I liked a busy social life, and enjoyed going out, so after my return to Sweden I accepted a few invitations. There were parties, and teas, and dances, and then the usual festive Swedish Christmas—sleigh rides in the icy winter snow, and mulled wine, family and friends. I tried not to think about Jack, but I did anyway, because I knew that what we had had together was much more than just a kiss. The practical side of me screamed that John Kennedy was a lost cause. But I couldn't shake him from my heart.

~

During the first week of the following March, before the spring thaw began to melt the snowdrifts, I came back to our apartment one day on Stockholm's Styrmansgatan, and as I brushed the white flakes off my coat, my mother came out from the sitting room and handed me a letter. "This arrived today," she told me. "From America. Washington."

I looked at the envelope, postmarked March 2, 1954, and then at the return address handwritten in the upper-left corner: RM 362, JFK, Senate Office Bldg., Washington, D.C.

Disbelief. JFK? For a moment, I wondered if this JFK were somebody else. But no. Not from the Senate in the capital of the United States. My heart was beating so loudly, I felt sure Mamma could hear it.

I opened the envelope slowly and carefully.

He asked if I remembered our time together in Cagnes. At the end, he wrote that, in September, he was planning to "return to France. . . . Will you be there?"

LOVE   LETTERS

I was amazed and thrilled that Jack had written to
me, that he had taken the time and trouble to look up
our address in Stockholm. I fully intended to write him
back, but in the meantime he had also found our telephone number and called the apartment, though unfortunately, when I wasn't there. My mother was at home
and spoke to him. Of course, she reported his calls to
me, but she wouldn't fill in many details. All she said
was, "Your Mr. Kennedy is full of charm." When I
asked what they talked about, she said, "We talked
about you. But not entirely."

On the following Tuesday, I missed him again.
"He's very persistent," Mamma said, smiling. "This is
his third call."

"Well, Mamma," I protested, "if you would just
ask him for a telephone number, I would—"

"Dear, I did ask him. He just says he'll call again."
My mother was quite precise, so I knew this had to be
true. Finally I sat down to write him, but in the midst
of writing the letter, he called and I was home.

"Gunilla? Is it you?" The long-distance wires
crackled, but I recognized that distinctive New Eng-

land voice. I was flooded with the same warm feeling that I'd experienced upon seeing him sitting in the banquette at Le Château that past August.

"Yes, Jack. How are you?"

"Just fine." He paused. I thought his voice sounded tentative, a little shy. I was pleased. "I might be coming back to Europe this summer."

I was thrilled to hear him say that. "That would be wonderful," I replied.

"Well, I'd want to see you, if that's possible?" He ended it like a question. I thought this was endearing.

"It's not impossible."

"Not impossible. Hmm. That's a start. Do you think we might meet in Paris?"

"Oh yes!" I began, and then put the brakes on. I wanted to see him again more than anything, but some instinct warned me to take it easy for now. "I mean, I don't know. I'm not planning to go there."

"The Riviera, then?"

"I'm not sure. I'm answering your letter now. I'll let you know."

"I'll write, too, when my plans are set. Okay?"

"Okay, Jack."

"I . . . well, I hope we can see each other. Really, Gunilla, I can't wait for us to meet again. Our evening together made me so happy. Good-bye."

We both had left so much unsaid, but I felt very emotional when I hung up the telephone. I went back to writing my letter. Having talked to him, however briefly, made me change the tone to sound more encouraging. I finished by saying that whatever we decided, I'd need to know when he was coming before making plans, since my mother and father, along with Ewa and me, and Anne Marie and her widowed mother, and an assortment of relatives, usually spent part of our summers in southern Sweden.

Only a week and a half passed, and then came another letter. He wrote that he was hoping to come to Europe in late August, asking if I would be busy, and if not, could we meet. He asked what I was doing, and if I planned to go back to Cagnes.

He finished by saying that he was thinking of leasing a boat. He dreamed of sailing ". . . the Mediterranean for two weeks—with you as crew."

I allowed my imagination to run free. I saw the two of us, alone in a big, beautiful yacht, white sails fluttering in the wind, with the crystal azure of the Mediterranean lapping all around us. I longed to be close to him again, to feel that exciting intimacy that had been so intense at Cap d'Antibes. The boat, the blue water, the idea of Jack and me alone at sea was romantic beyond belief. I knew, however, that Jack had a wife and that I shouldn't be having this dream. But every time I pushed this vision away, it crept back, invading my heart.

And then there was something else that concerned me. My fragile heart muscle from the typhoid was still a problem. As a result, I often felt tired. Was I vivacious enough for the dashing Jack Kennedy?

Knowing that Jack would call or write soon, I gave a lot of thought to the best way to arrange our reunion. That much I knew—whatever the location, I really wanted to see him again. I even discussed it with my mother and Ewa.

Ewa was a bit younger than I, but she was more secure. For one thing, she had already been married—to Anne Marie's brother, Ernst Linder (in our particular Swedish family circle, everyone is intimately acquainted with all their relatives—or else they *are* your relatives). Although her marriage had been short-lived, I thought her opinion on the subject of my seeing Jack would be more worldly than mine.

"First of all, I don't think you should go anywhere to meet him unless it's mutual ground," Ewa pronounced.

Well, I wasn't planning to go to America. Or the Riveria, either. That was still his territory. His family went there.

Ewa agreed.

"He's always talking about Paris," I added, as the melody of "I Love Paris" drifted through my mind.

Ewa became contemplative. "That might make sense," she decided.

"If Jack is so anxious to see me, he should come here to Sweden, to meet my family. It's a little more proper."

Mamma was not particularly liberal, even by Swedish or European standards, and this was not only a different era, it was a different cultural climate. We did not need endless discussions to remind us that Jack had a wife. It seemed to my family that his pursuit of me might mean his marriage was not a solid one. We didn't reflect upon why or how.

Mamma put it her way: "I cannot say I approve of this, Gunilla, but who is to say what is right? You are a grown-up woman now, and you will do what you must. But I advise you to think very carefully about this before you go jumping into something just because your heart tells you to. Use your head."

This was going to be a struggle. I already feared it would be my head that would lose.

My father, Olof von Post, preferred to leave such discussions to the women of the house. He was almost two decades older than Mamma, and I, too, preferred men more mature than I was. But my Pappa, Olle, whose lineage went far back into Swedish history, was actually rather artistic and romantic, and I inherited these qualities. Pappa knew a great deal about politics and geneology, as well as painting and the arts, and he often took me out for Sunday walks in the park, stopping at galleries along the way. He also sponsored several young artists over the years.

My mother was a proud woman of her generation. She believed in duty to husband and family, and she was a great hostess, with an extraordinary sense of humor, and wasn't at all like her bohemian mother. And although we shared certain sensibilities, I wasn't like her. I remember back when I was in my teens, one of the men I'd met at a social tea, Carl-Gustaf Tersmeden, became quite interested in me. He was a charming and generous bon vivant. He got to know my mother, too, and one day he said to her, while looking at me, "Mrs. von Post, why do you suppose the apple has fallen so far from the tree?"

This mother/daughter difference must have been part of our heritage. As I've said, my maternal grandmother, Karin (the bohemian, poetry-writing original who disapproved of men who preferred soft drinks to champagne), was artistic, funny, and unconventional. I learned early on that although there was lots of nobility in my background, fortunately it had been mixed up with some refreshing new blood from the west coast!

Pappa's ancestors were originally from Schaumburg, Germany, where their name was simply Post, appearing for the first time, as far as we can tell, in 1205. The von Posts came to Sweden in the seventeenth century, and most of the men were soldiers.

One of the more distinguished descendants of what we consider another branch of the family was Laurens van der Post, who died in December of 1996 at age ninety. Laurens was not only a soldier, but an explorer and author and, perhaps most famously, Prince Charles's mentor, as well as the godfather to his son Prince William.

In the family tradition, my father began his career as an officer in the Swedish military. Back in the 1930s, he was about to be offered an important promotion, a position at the Royal Court, but pomp and circumstance were not for Olle (another trait we shared), so later he took an entirely different route and became the head of the Swedish branch of Motor Union, a British automobile insurance company with offices in Gamla Stan, Stockholm's old city. I have often thought that my mother would have delighted in being the wife of an important Court officer, but she had married a man who was just too independent in spirit. Of course, that was one reason I adored him so.

Pappa wasn't entirely silent on the subject of my courtship, however. He did speak discreetly with our cousin Eric von Post, who was Sweden's ambassador to

Warsaw. Eric had a wide view, as did my father, of world politics. "John Kennedy," he said, "is a very charming and ambitious young man, with an even more ambitious father." If the tone of Eric's pronouncement was ominous, I was not going to let it scare me off.

Beginning in mid-June, Jack began calling again. I was working for the Swedish Royal Automobile Club. The club's offices were located next to the Grand Hotel, which is still the leading luxury hotel in all of Scandinavia. The Royal Automobile Club has an imposing redbrick facade, and all the flags of the northern nations fly from high on its rooftop. It's a wonderful location, overlooking the fleet of ferryboats that take people to and from the archipelago in the Baltic, and it is directly across the water from the Royal Palace. I enjoyed the work, although it didn't involve much more than smiling, giving people advice, and handing out brochures. I did it well. I had told Jack to try to telephone me in the evenings, after work, but not too late. The six-hour time difference allowed him to place the calls from his office rather than from his home.

"Gunilla, my dear."

Hearing that, I knew my heart was winning.

"I don't have any news yet about my trip. I just wanted to hear your voice." His own voice was more comfortable now, more confident. Our talks and letters had reassured him that our feelings for each other were not only shared but were blossoming into something neither of us could stop.

"Hearing your voice is wonderful for me, too," I said.

"But I *am* going to Europe. It just will have to be a little later. In the fall. Do you think you could come down to the Côte d'Azur?"

"Well . . ."

"Okay. How about Paris?"

"Maybe." I was beginning to weaken. Actually, the truth was I was so vulnerable to his entreaties, that even if he had said Tahiti, Siberia, or the Australian outback, I feared I might say yes. But I wanted to remain careful, so I answered, "Jack, I really must think about this."

"You do want us to get together, don't you?" he said, his voice full of ardor.

"Yes," I answered quickly. "Oh yes. We will work it out. I'll write you tomorrow. I can't wait to see you again."

I picked up my fountain pen the next day. I am almost certain that it was in this long letter that I told Jack a little anecdote from my childhood: "You remember my friend Anne Marie Linder? The other day she reminded me that her father made a remark about me when I was a child of seven: 'This little girl is going to become very dangerous to men!' " The remainder of the letter I filled with news and a little gossip, but the most important part was that I gave in a little about our meeting place. I felt braver since I now had an ally in Ewa. "I can't promise anything yet," I wrote him. "But we might try for Paris."

During his next call, Jack said, "I don't know if you are still dangerous, but I'm trying like hell to find out!" Then he suggested another compromise: He would go to Cap d'Antibes and then travel from there to meet me in Paris.

But he could be stubborn. He held on to the idea of the Riviera like an Irish setter with a mutton bone. In the letter that followed, he repeated his plans to travel to Europe in the fall, and pleaded with me to meet him in Paris or the Riviera, adding that he didn't want to "drift through Europe" and especially he didn't want to wait for word "from the North that never comes."

I wrote back, telling him that if we could work out all the details, I would meet him in Paris. We made tentative plans to meet there in September.

In August, I received an urgently romantic phone call: "I see your face everywhere, and sometimes you come to me in dreams. I can't tell you how badly I want to see you, but you will understand how much when we meet. You know how I yearn to be in Paris? Well, that's how much I yearn to be with you."

I longed for September, but on the third of that

month, a telegram arrived from Hyannisport. He said he had hurt his leg, but worse, that he was in the hospital. His trip would have to be rescheduled and he would send another letter. He ended with "TRIP POSTPONED. MANY REGRETS—JOHN"

The cable upset me, not only because Jack had injured his leg—I knew how active he liked to be, despite his back—but because I had been looking forward to our reunion so eagerly. The idea of not seeing him again made me feel hollow, and my disappointment had no boundaries.

Since the telegram had come from Hyannisport, I wrote back to him there. But I heard nothing for a week, two weeks, and then a month. By October I became alarmed. I'm grateful that I didn't know what Jack's real troubles were until much later. Although he may well have hurt his leg, what really happened was that shortly after contacting me, he was flown to New York, to the Hospital for Special Surgery, for an operation on his back. If pressed, Jack would explain casually that he'd ruptured his lower lumbar disc while playing football at Harvard, which was true, but he also had Addison's disease—an adrenal malfunction—and that was a secret. The operation was a double-fusion procedure, and he barely survived it. If I'd known he was given last rites, I would have been frantic. I was spared that, but I was to find out that al-

though the operation was fairly successful, his conva-
lescence was going to take many months, and the pain
would endure the rest of his life.

Finally, but not until November, a letter arrived. He
was still in the hospital after two months, and terribly
disappointed not to have been able to come to Europe.
He expected to stay in the hospital for another month,
then return to Washington after the New Year and
remain there until the congressional break in mid-
summer.

There was a postscript: ". . . any chance you will be
coming to the U.S.?"

People usually send flowers, chocolates, or at least
a get-well card to loved ones in the hospital. I wanted
to send myself, to book passage on the next ship to
New York. I wanted to be by his bedside, to comfort
him and reassure him. Wouldn't it show him how
much I cared if I made such a journey?

Instead, I sent him a long letter and tried to express
in words what I felt. I told him of my frustration at not
being near him while he was in such terrible discomfort. I said that my heart was near breaking for him,
and that I prayed for him in my own special way.

His response arrived on Christmas Eve. He said
that beneath my beautiful, yet reserved "face that still
haunts me—beats a warm heart."

That was what Jack needed the most. A warm heart. He had so many responsibilities on his shoulders—his position in the Senate, his father's overwhelming ambitions for him, his unfulfilling home life. He needed someone to lean on, to share his burdens with—someone who would love him for his weaknesses as well as his strengths. I don't think anybody in his family had ever given him that kind of unconditional love.

I knew in the depths of my being that this was exactly the kind of love I could give him, and that he would give back to me. My days and nights were invaded by thoughts of him. He seemed to miss me as terribly as I missed him. He asked why I didn't arrange for the Automobile Club to send me to the States so that I could show American travelers the glories of Sweden.

He was leaving the hospital for good in a few days, then going to Palm Beach for a couple of months with his family to recuperate, returning to Washington at the end of July. He then hoped to come back to Cagnes. He signed the letter, "Your—Jack."

I was touched by his constant mention of Cagnes and the Côte d'Azur. I could still remember my exact feelings at the doorway of La Bourgade when he kissed me that last time, brushed my hair aside, and left. Bittersweet though that moment was, it was my unconscious elusiveness that must have done the trick. I had turned him down, and Jack Kennedy wasn't used to that.

He called one night and started talking about our lying on a beach together in Italy. I didn't say yes and I didn't say no, but I was learning to stick to my guns. I discovered that Jack wasn't the kind of man you could tell what to do, but if he thought something was his idea, that was different. I had just seen an American musical movie in which Donald O'Connor sang, "A man chases a girl until she catches him." That was good advice.

At the end of our conversation, he said, "Gunilla, if you have a photo of yourself, please send it to me. Send me as many as you can. I need to see your face."

If I had once wanted to rush blindly into his arms wherever he was, I now became more determined than ever to arrange our next encounter myself, to ask him to come to Sweden the following summer. Mamma was right. If he desired our reunion urgently enough—as much as I did—he would cross the ocean and come visit me here.

I wrote him on the letterhead of the Royal Automobile Club, saying that I hoped he would sail to Europe in the summer, and invited him to visit us in Båstad in the southern part of Sweden.

Mid-March, his response arrived. He said he would

be visiting Indochina and Formosa when the Senate adjourned in July, but first he was coming to Europe. Still obsessed with the Riviera, he wanted me to suggest an Italian beach where we could relax and watch the surf roll in for a couple of weeks. He never stopped mentioning the Automobile Club and wondered, "if I join" would I plan his itinerary? He promised that he would "not fail to come—and you?"

By the summer of 1955, I was working as a hostess at the Snäckgärdsbaden Hotel near Visby, on the Swedish island of Gotland. In between behaving like a perfect young lady with the guests and helping out at the gift shop, I wrote another letter to America and suggested that Jack look up my friend Mona Boheman, the daughter of our ambassador to Washington. I also sent my Gotland address and promised to include my photo next time, taken in front of the Stockholm apartment building, hinting that even though he still seemed obsessed with southern France or Italy, Sweden *did* have its pleasures. I added a postscript, because he liked to do that in his letters, too: "By the way, you seem to think Sweden is cold and damp. Well, if you visit us in the southern part in August, you'll see we actually have sunlight and nice warm breezes!"

He responded, and his resolve about the location of our reunion had cracked somewhat. He'd be finished in Washington on August 1, and considered coming to

Europe on or about the twelfth. He said that if I were going to be in Sweden, then he would travel to our country, adding that he hoped we had beaches there.

But then, inevitably, he brought up Italy again, suggesting that if I decided to go to the Italian Riviera, he would join me.

Continuing, he admitted that he had not met my friend Mona Boheman yet, but if he did, he was going to ask her if she knew "a beautiful Swedish girl with a quiet smile" who lived on a mountaintop in the South of France at the end of the summer, 1953.

I finally convinced him that if we were to meet at all, it was going to be in Sweden. With some reluctance—and the usual undercurrents of complaints about Scandinavian weather—he capitulated by mail in July: "my plans are your plans" and that he would give up the warmth of the Côte d'Azur for Scandinavia, even though, he said, I had once told him that the summers here were "cold and damp."

I don't believe I had *quite* put it that way, but either way, I was terribly excited about the prospect of seeing him again. He told me he was planning to leave by ship on July 27, then drive from Le Havre "to Sweden and you." He then, yet again, suggested that if I did—after all—want to go to Italy in late summer, he would need a guide from the Automobile Club, preferably me.

His postscript said: "And don't forget the photo."

So I went immediately to the photo shop and had a copy made of a picture taken of me in front of Styrmansgatan and sent it, along with another snapshot of Visby, the site of my summer job.

Mid-June came his response. Thanking me for the picture of Visby, and, he added, for "your photograph, which I liked best of all." His plans had changed a bit again, and now he was either coming to me on July 29, sailing on the *Ile de France* and arriving August 5, or on board the *United States*, arriving on the tenth.

Jack closed with another tug at my heartstrings, writing that although he feared it might be "a long way to Gunilla—it is worth it."

I now truly believed that nothing would keep us apart—not the wide Atlantic Ocean, nor his domestic situation, nor the pressures of his career. Deep inside, I knew that our destiny was to be together.

Even with that belief, I found it almost impossible to relax, because I wanted him so. When the telephone rang, I froze in anticipation, and when it wasn't Jack, I was disappointed. But often enough, it was Jack, and often enough, there was a letter waiting for me when I arrived home. I reread many of them and savored the words he managed to put down on paper, but knew that the real meaning was between the lines.

On a cool but sunny June morning, I ran to our mail slot at the front door. Among the envelopes on the parquet floor was one that made me rejoice. That now-familiar handwriting and the American postage stamps were beautiful to see. I tore open the envelope in the foyer. He said he thought I looked "well and happy" in the snapshot I'd sent him.

Congress was adjourning on August 5. He had booked passage on the *United States* after all, docking at Le Havre on the tenth. He would be in Sweden on the twelfth, he said, and he asked me to confirm my address in Båstad (which he spelled "Bastaad").

He wrote that it was 101 degrees in Washington. He ended by saying he was "anxious to leave and to see my Swedish friend."

S W E D E N

It had been nearly two years since Jack and I met, and by June of 1955, he had sent me many letters and made twice as many telephone calls.

He called me again in July: "I'm pretty sure I'm still leaving on the *United States* in the first week of August. I'll confirm with you."

"I hope it's true, Jack. I couldn't stand another delay. How are you? I mean, really how are you?"

He started to answer with his usual upbeat confidence. "Don't worry. I'm better." But then his voice changed. I had talked to him enough to know that he was exposing something about himself he would rather not have revealed. "I—well, I should tell you that I have to use crutches sometimes, but that won't last."

I was anguished for him. But I had to ask: "Does it hurt, Jack?"

There was a silence. "Every now and then. But it's not so bad. When I think about you it doesn't hurt at all."

There, he'd done it again. He made me feel so special. "Ohh, Jack . . ." If he couldn't see my smile, he could hear it.

He added, "You know, Gunilla, we're both going to be a bit nervous. It's been a while."

I agreed, but I didn't dare let him know just how nervous I was.

"But I have to see you. I need to."

"Me, too, Jack."

"I can't wait. I'll send you the dates as soon as I get them."

"Good. Take real good care of yourself, Jack. Bye-bye. And a big hug."

"Good-bye, my Gunilla."

The wire went dead. I sat by the telephone, savoring his voice, wondering how he would look, imagining myself in his arms, his lips upon mine. I went to bed and dreamed.

The next morning I sent him the address of Sjöstugan, where we always stayed in Båstad in August. I promised him that as soon as I was actually certain his cabin had been booked on the ship, I would give my notice to Hasse Bratt, the manager of the Snäckgärdsbaden Hotel, and that I would leave the island of Gotland and fly up to Stockholm for a week before meeting him in Båstad.

But Jack, being as self-assured and clearly as determined as he was, just assumed that I would accept his plans as a fait accompli—because he went right ahead and sent his confirmation letter to me at Styrmansgatan

45! As usual, he made up his own Swedish spelling
("Skyransgatan"), and as usual, I got it anyway.
Mamma read it to me over the phone:

He estimated his arrival in Sweden would be on the
twelfth. He was bringing a friend, a Mr. MacDonald,
with him, and asked me to book a couple of rooms for
them. He said he couldn't read my Swedish so clearly,
but that he knew he'd be able to find me, no matter
what, ". . . of that I am *sure*. Until we meet—Jack."

I marched right into Mr. Bratt's office and resigned.
He gave me a stern look and complained that I hadn't
given him enough notice. I liked Hasse Bratt very
much; he looked like Richard Burton and had the same
sort of charm. I told him some little white lie about my
reasons for leaving (I was not going to say it was because I was going to meet my American from Boston!),
and—because I was so excited and happy—I threw my
arms around him and said, "You are so wonderful, Mr.
Bratt!" His disappointment ended, and he said I'd done
a great job. In fact, he even gave me a going-away
party.

After that, I embarked immediately for Stockholm
to load up on more summer clothes. I called the big
Skånegården Hotel in Båstad to reserve Jack's two
rooms; they said they were fully booked, but would
keep me in mind if a cancellation came up. In a week, I
was on my way to Båstad to join my family.

Båstad is very beautiful, even when it is cool and rainy (Jack's persistent fear). It's on a little peninsula of southwestern Sweden that juts out into the ocean, or actually the Kattegat, an arm of the North Sea between Sweden and Denmark, only about seventy miles away. The Davis Cup tennis tournament is still held in Båstad in July, next to Sjöstugan, high above a panorama of colorful sailboats set against a sheen of sparkling blue sea.

By August, the tournament was over and the crowds had left, but an aftermath of excitement remained in the air. As I gazed at the hills and the sweep of water below, the thought occurred to me that this was not unlike Italy, or the French Riviera, and that by my insisting that Jack come to me, instead of my meeting him in southern Europe, we were both getting what we wanted.

I went directly to Sjöstugan, which in Swedish means, literally, "the sea cottage." Sjöstugan was built around 1910, and its style echoed Swedish country architecture all the way back to the 1700s—a substantially constructed large stone house, surrounded by lawns and rose gardens, with a huge pillored terrace overlooking the water. It was owned by our old friend Vera Leijonhufvud; we had rented rooms from her there for many summers. The Linders also stayed there each August, and Anne Marie and her mother, General

Linder's widow, whom we called Aunt Wiveka, or "the Generalskan," had already arrived by the time I got there. As soon as we were settled, I called the Skånegården, but they still didn't have space. There wasn't a single room to be had, I was told, let alone two separate ones for Jack and his friend Mr. MacDonald.

I tested my newfound independent spirit. "But you must find *something*," I argued. "These are very important Americans coming from Washington, D.C.!" The stubborn, urgent sound of my voice must have impressed the manager, because he finally said, "Well, we do have the new addition, adjacent to the main building." It turned out that he had two rooms available in this modern wing, nice but not fancy. I reserved them right away. I was pleased, really, because this was even more secluded, surely more discreet.

On the same day, I received a telegram, sent from aboard the USS *United States*.

A BIENTOT

JACK

I was enormously touched. I also began to relax. This was the gesture of a man in love, the kind of thing that lovers do for each other, and I knew it down to my bones. Now I had less fear and apprehension. He said the ship would dock at Le Havre on the tenth and he'd be here about the twelfth. It was going to be an endless two days.

On the first day I took long walks by the sea. I swam. I tried to sleep. I rode my horse, Nestor, over the hills. The next day was the same. I couldn't bear to sit around, so I went to the hairdresser, and then out again, this time for an even longer trek along the water and then through the fields. I returned to the house on the afternoon of the eleventh pleasantly exhausted.

Aunt Wiveka, looking a bit flushed and excited, said to me, "You had two American friends here looking for you, asking 'Where is Gunilla von Post?' and I said 'Gunilla von Post is not here! Gunilla is out!' so they—"

I didn't bother to hear anything else. They were a whole day early! I was beside myself with excitement. I ran as fast as I could to the Skånegården, and around to the annex. They had just arrived at that moment, and there was Jack in khaki pants and a blue polo shirt. He was with another man, who was much larger and husky, and they were both surrounded by suitcases.

I rushed toward Jack, my heart pounding, and fell into his arms. We held each other tightly. I was so happy to see him. No words could express my feelings.

Quickly, he asked, "Gunilla, where have you been? I've been looking for you everywhere!"

I was glad he'd been searching for me. So I said, "Good!" still hugging him. A suntan tinted his lightly freckled face, and he looked even more handsome than I remembered, his youth and *joie de vivre* shining from within.

He introduced me to Torby—"Mr. MacDonald"— and then said, with his eyes and his smile still directed at me, "Torby, would you take the bags?" Torby disappeared instantly with the bags. And then Jack led me into his room.

Inside, he swung the door shut so eagerly that it banged, and I fell into his arms. I gave in totally to my emotions. He kissed me so that it seemed as if we had seen each other only yesterday. I didn't hesitate or think about anything except the two of us.

From the very beginning, I could tell he wanted desperately to please me, and I felt the same. Jack was gentle and caring, and his love was as sweet as his kisses and caresses had been on the Riviera. The connection I had felt at Le Château and on Eden Roc was now a hundred times deeper.

This wasn't a man who simply needed a woman to

satisfy his cravings and would then go on to something else. This was a man who had moved heaven and earth, taken risks that even then could have been fatal to his career, and traveled halfway around the world to be with me, and now we were sweeping each other into a whirlwind of passion, as if now that we had touched each other again, we could not separate.

I was relatively inexperienced, and Jack's tenderness was a revelation. He said, "Gunilla, we've waited two years for this. It seems almost too good to be true, and I want to make you happy." For the first time, I could let go and luxuriate in the attentions of a man who not only respected and cared for me but clearly loved me. I fully trusted him.

I knew I must be gentle and careful, too. His back trouble was always a critical factor. Jack made love with his hands, with his marvelous, healthy Irish skin, with his mouth—with everything.

We were wonderfully *sensual*. There were times when just the stillness of being together was thrilling enough. Sometimes we whispered to each other, too, and sometimes we giggled a bit. But whether he was talking or silent, Jack's eyes always laughed. Even when we had to slow down because of his back, he was smiling.

Being with him was so astounding that I thought at

one point, Am I crazy? But the answer was obvious: No, I'm happy. We allowed ourselves an intensity that was breathtaking. When he looked at me and said, "I love you. I can't believe this is happening—that I'm with you again," I saw tears in his eyes, and I knew we were meant for each other. And underneath it all, I felt comfortable, secure, and safe. I was loved, and I loved.

Later, I put my head on his shoulder. I looked up at his face, inches away from mine. I told him, softly, "I'm very happy, Jack." I kissed his cheek. "Thank you for coming back to me."

He smiled, with his eyes closed. "I'm happy, too, Gunilla. I feel as though I've been set free." Then we drifted off into sweet sleep.

~

I have thought many times about that incredible moment when Jack returned to me, and wondered just what were all the elements that came together so magically to create such a once-in-a-lifetime occasion. I never realized it when it was happening, but now I know that not only did I fall in love with him, I fell in love with America, which seemed exotic, wild and fascinating, just as John Kennedy was. But there was something else. Years later, when I learned the truth about his hospitalization and near-death in 1954, during the months he was writing and calling me as our long-distance courtship grew, I believe he genuinely thought he might never see me again. But he survived, and we did meet again, so it was even more precious. It was a miracle for both of us.

～

On Saturday evening, we made up quite a merry group for dinner at the Strand restaurant next to the Skånegården, a beautiful, spacious room overlooking the harbor, with good food and wine, music, and dancing. Our table consisted of Jack and me; Ewa; Anne Marie and her new husband, Curt Engelbrecht; her mother, Aunt Wiveka; my friend Madelaine Lindesvärd and her husband, Bo, and parents, Mr. and Mrs. Muhl; and Torby MacDonald. Torby—his large frame not at all unattractive—was darker than Jack, but just as big-hearted. He turned out to be most amusing, too. He and Jack had been roommates at Harvard and had played on the varsity football team together —Torby, eventually, was captain. The two of them were always bantering with each other, telling jokes and anecdotes that inevitably ended in hearty laughter. Fifteen years out of college, they were still a good team.

Jack came in on crutches. His back problem was

chronic, and sometimes it was worse than better. That night it was a little worse, but by the time he sat down at the table, mostly everybody forgot about his physical troubles and just enjoyed him.

Although Jack's entrance with me caused a bit of a stir, I really didn't care too much what people thought. I assumed people who knew me well enough didn't have to be told that I was in love. It has always been almost impossible for me to hide my emotions. My eyes and my voice show everything.

They could have just watched and seen it all, anyway. At the table, Jack and I were unusually affectionate. He punctuated some of his remarks by giving my hand a squeeze. Once or twice he leaned over and whispered in my ear, often something funny and wicked that he didn't want others to hear.

Madelaine Lindesvärd, whose father was a famous Gothenburg lawyer, was very intelligent and often quite funny. She was fascinated by Jack and hung on his every word. More than once, I caught her staring at him intensely across the table. Jack noticed, too, and eventually, with all his abundant charm, he said to her, "Madelaine, there is something on your mind. I can tell."

Madelaine was one of the most self-assured girls I knew, so no blush colored her cheeks, as would have happened had it been me. She smiled and said steadily, "Oh, Mr. Kennedy, there is always something on my mind."

Jack waved his finger at her, like a wise school-teacher, and said, "You'd better be careful. I can read other people's thoughts, you know."

With her eyes cast downward, Madelaine replied, "Well, then, I'm afraid I really must beg your pardon."

After the laughter died down around the table, Jack said to me under his breath, in his own version of a Swedish accent, "Not so pret-ty, but *very* wit-ty!"

Anne Marie's mother, Aunt Wiveka, was seated directly opposite us. Two chairs away was Anne Marie—blond like me, but rounder and with a Scandinavian charm. We were, that night, in short dinner dresses.

I sat between Jack and Torby. Jack made a point of conversing with everybody, and found something personal to say to them all. He positively radiated warmth, pulling everyone into his aura like a bright lantern attracts the creatures of the night. Jack was seductive; he rarely missed a chance to flirt with all the women, our mothers included. But he cast a spell on people that I've never quite seen before or since. And everyone—man, woman, child—was smitten, and happy to be near him.

"Anne Marie and I are, of course, old friends,"

Jack said across the table to her mother. Beautiful in her youth, Aunt Wiveka was now imposingly large, a result of her devotion to good food and wine, and chocolates. She looked like a ship in full sail.

Jack directed his attention to Anne Marie. "We had such a good time that evening in France, didn't we?"

"Yes," Anne Marie said demurely. "It was a very special evening."

"Like tonight!" Jack said. And then back to Aunt Wiveka. "I remember how pretty your daughter was then, and now she's even lovelier," he told her.

Aunt Wiveka said, "Why, thank you," and spread some pâté on a piece of toast and ate it happily.

I turned to Jack and said, softly, "That was nice of you. Anne Marie does look pretty tonight."

Torby looked at Anne Marie. "Yes, she really is pretty," he said. He turned to Aunt Wiveka and said, "Your daughter must take after her father." Aunt Wiveka almost fell off of her chair.

In spite of Jack's habit of trying to throw French phrases into his speech, his taste in cuisine was basically all-American. When the Strand waiter turned to him for his order, he said, "Just a steak, please," and the waiter nodded and left.

A little while later when our meals began to arrive, the waiter placed a tournedos, swathed in *sauce bearnaise,* in front of Jack. "No, no," he said. "Just a steak.

You know? An American steak." The waiter removed his plate. He returned with a filet mignon, with a large puddle of herbed butter dripping over the top. "Excuse me," Jack said, slightly impatient now. "You see, what I'd like is a plain, American, *clean,* broiled steak, you understand?"

It was uncertain whether the waiter understood.

Jack tried again. "Look," he began, really somewhat annoyed. "You take a piece of beef, a good piece of meat, and you just—I don't know—you just throw it under, or over, a fire, get it sort of crusty outside, turn it over, and *bring it to me!*"

Just to be sure, I translated. Jack got what he wanted. I wondered if he always did.

Svend Asmussen's orchestra was in residence at the Strand, and they were very popular. In fact, the Danish Asmussen was a prominent bandleader for many decades to come in Sweden. In 1955, his music was dreamy and romantic. After dinner, Jack's strength returned, and leaving his crutches at the table, he asked me to dance. I wondered if they would play "I Love Paris," but they didn't. No matter. I just enjoyed the moment, the evening, and the promise of what was to come.

When the party broke up in the early hours of the morning, Torby, Jack, and I walked outside together and headed toward their rooms. On the way, Jack looked up to the sky. It was a crystal-clear night. His face broke into that smile, and he said, "Look at the stars. The *stars,* Gunilla. The *stars!*" Jack would say this several times during the week, and I began to share his wonder at this nightly, glittering show in the sky. When we arrived at the annex, Torby went to bed, and I stayed with Jack.

Jack Kennedy awakened something in me that was new, and every day, no matter what activity we engaged in—swimming, lazy lunches and festive dinners, meeting with my friends and family, short walks in the gardens, driving through the countryside—we both felt a special pulse all day long, because we knew that soon, after nightfall, we would be in each other's arms again.

That night after dinner began an unspoken pattern. Although it was a tiny heartbreak each time, after being together we parted and I went back to Sjöstugan.

Torby knew of our love, and keeping such a high flame invisible to others wasn't really possible. But Torby was a good chaperone, besides being a loyal and loving friend to Jack. In fact, it was Torby, and Torby alone, who slipped some clues about Jack's unhappy marriage, although during his entire visit, Jack never mentioned it. But one afternoon, when Jack was resting, Torby said to me, "Just watching the way Jack is with you, I don't know—it's funny. He's never that way with his wife. He's written you all those letters, but I don't think he's even sent her a card."

I didn't want to say anything, but I did. "Well, I think she must love him. She seems to be kind to him."

"Oh, she came to visit him in the hospital, but I don't think she was that concerned. I've known Jack since we were nineteen years old, and I've never seen him quite this happy."

"Torby, let's go to Jack's room and plan the rest of your visit."

~

Happily, we had a whole week ahead of us. We enjoyed the sunshine, and I marveled at Jack's abandon and the fun he had while swimming in the bay below Sjöstugan. But I'm afraid he overdid it that first Sunday, because in the afternoon he was in such pain that it broke my heart. After a late lunch, Jack and I set off for an afternoon drive, but made it only as far as the village of Båstad.

"We're going to have to stop, Gunilla," he said, and when I looked at him, the tension in his eyes told me how severely he was suffering. "Please, Gunilla, you have to get me some painkillers. I've run out, and I can't go on without some medication."

I had never before seen anyone in such physical misery. He looked washed out, even under his tan. I was frightened, but absolutely determined to find a way to help him. Fortunately, he had a prescription from an American doctor, and he gave it to me. "Wait here," I said, and darted out of the car.

As I rushed out into the street, I realized I had seen Jack at the height of pleasure and in the depths of pain in only a few days. If the former was magnificent and unforgettable, the latter terrified me. I ran faster, tripping over the cobblestones, to the nearest chemist's, an old-fashioned Dickensian-looking shop on a little side street. The faded green shade was pulled down across the beveled-glass windows at the entrance. It was already late Sunday afternoon, but the proprietor happened to be inside. I banged on the door, nearly breaking the panes, until he unlocked it.

The chemist looked at me, the door ajar, and said, "I'm sorry, we're closed."

Out of breath and near tears myself, I edged my way into the shop and shouted, "I'm sorry, too, but this is an emergency and I must get this filled right away!"

I handed him the prescription. The chemist stared at the piece of paper, then pushed his spectacles down and stared at me over the frames. He shook his head. "I don't know . . . This is very strong medicine. And this is a foreign doctor . . ."

"But you don't understand," I said. "This is an

American senator, visiting Sweden for a week. He is staying with us. He was hurt during the war, he is a hero. This is a terrible back injury and it's suddenly so serious, we have nowhere to turn. You must help us. We need help! I must entreat you to help us!"

It worked. I was willing to drop to my knees and beg if necessary, but I didn't have to, probably because the anguish in my eyes and the pleading in my voice were so convincing.

I took what the chemist gave me and ran back to Jack, who was being brave about his pain, but there was a film of perspiration across his forehead and a tight expression on his face. "Oh, thank you, thank you, dearest," he said, trying to embrace me with gratitude. "This won't take long." He swallowed a couple of the pills and we sat quietly for a while. Soon he was better, and we continued our drive.

Looking back, I believe that Jack possessed his own extraordinary kind of spiritual strength. He was in constant pain, and he could only have summoned such courage from heaven to combat the unrelenting physical torture he lived with each and every day. Most people with such pain could be forgiven a retreat into private suffering, but Jack fought his pain head on. He embraced life with ferocious energy; instead of living in bitter seclusion, he became the most charismatic president of the United States. Whether he would ever have admitted it or not, I'm convinced that he did it with God's help.

I've often wondered if his need for painkillers was also connected to his need for me. The unspoken fear of our romance coming to an end was further incentive for him to dull his aching body in order to fully focus on being with me as often as he could.

Despite Jack's pain, he had relaxed the moment he saw me. He was away from his father, the pressures of Washington, the competitive traditions of his family. For the first time, he had the freedom to be himself, and I think he needed that freedom desperately. He had sacrificed most of his life to please old Joe Kennedy, but that seemed far away while he was in Sweden. Here, for those glorious moments we had together, his life was his own, and he was able to feel—and to love—with a depth and honesty he might never be allowed again.

~

As luck would have it, Jack's visit coincided with one of those moments in our Swedish summer when nature explodes with great lush flowers and trees, when the ocean takes on a special sparkle and the air is crisp and clean. Our warm season is so short that the natives rejoice in it like creatures who have been hiding in caves all winter, only to burst forth into the sun for whatever time the old Norse gods have granted them.

On one of the most beautiful of those days, my cousin Ambassador Eric von Post and his wife hosted a luncheon/reception in honor of my aunt's fiftieth birthday at their summer house, Svalgården, and I brought Jack and Torby. The garden was at the peak of bloom, virtually everyone we knew in Båstad was there, and the food was fresh from the sea and surrounding farms.

Although Jack was his usual sunny self and the picture of 1950s American casual—Bermuda shorts and a blue Lacoste polo shirt—he was relieved when he spotted a big hammock strung between two of the apple trees. "Eric," he asked quietly of my cousin, "do you mind if I lie in this for a bit?" The answer was "Of course, not at all." Jack whispered to me, "It helps my back." I rocked him to and fro, which he liked, and his magnetism drew all the guests to his side. He charmed everyone from a horizontal position. "With his crutches and handsome face," Cousin Margaretha von Post said, "Jack looks both young and old at the same time."

One morning I went horseback riding and Jack photographed me on Nestor. Later, we took a tour through the beautiful botanical gardens called Norrvikens—members of Alfred Nobel's family lived there—and looked at the array of subtropical flowers. As with everything else during his visit, Jack seemed to drink in all the sights, sounds, and fragrances with a healthy thirst for beauty and new experiences. He was curious about everything.

As the days went on, Jack became especially attentive to my mother, and in fact the two of them often had private chats. Besides being warm, Mamma was candid and direct, and the two of them got along together beautifully. Once I asked him what they talked about, and he smiled mischievously, saying, "Well, Brita and I have quite a bit to discuss." I asked if they talked about me. "Sometimes," he said, and then we were off on another adventure.

By midweek, Jack, Torby, and I decided to drive their rental car wherever the mood took us, although I think Jack was still trusting that my earlier experiences at the Royal Automobile Club would guide our wheels. I had more faith in the weather than they did, and would have voted for a convertible, but Jack was still searching the skies for clouds, so they'd leased a coupe. As it happened, the elements remained benign during their entire stay.

We traveled all across Skåne, Sweden's southernmost province. Skåne is like a different country, and is dotted with more than two hundred castles and manor

houses, along with quaint old eighteenth-century farm-
houses and thatched-roof cottages, across a landscape
of fields and meadows. Although not quite as hilly as
Ireland, the countryside resembled his ancestral home-
land, and Jack loved it.

It was like driving with two enthusiastic kids, with
great outbursts of laughter and an intense curiosity
about everything we passed. There is a very particular
kind of all-American energy that I found foreign and
enticing, and these two had it in abundance. "What's
that?" I would hear, usually from Jack. "Let's stop and
take a look!" And we usually did.

Jack always took the wheel, often driving with one
hand while his other arm was around me, and Torby
sat on the outside. Sometimes I put my arms around
both of them. And Jack sang.

He sang "I Love Paris"—constantly!—all the way
across southwestern Sweden. At first we took day trips
and returned each night to Båstad. By the end of the
week, even I could sing nearly every stanza of "I Love
Paris."

One day, as we approached Torekov, a small fishing
village, Torby turned to me and said, "I've never seen
Jack so happy!" and hugged my shoulders.

We pulled to a stop in the little main street. "This
looks like Cape Cod!" exclaimed Jack, with the expression of a boy who has just unwrapped a favorite gift on

Christmas morning. He was finding Sweden familiar and warm.

"Cape Cod?" I asked.

"Remember when I wrote you from our place at Hyannisport? That's Cape Cod. Years ago, the Cape was all about fishing."

I understood. And I suppose they were similar. In sharp, vivid contrast to the verdant landscape of Skåne, the coastal villages offer cozy harbor scenes of boats and nets strung out to dry, small colorful houses and jetties, and air pungent with that salt-sea smell that always makes my heart feel light.

Several of my good friends and family from Stockholm had summer houses in Torekov, and so we were grandly entertained and fed by them—first some schnapps, then sole, shrimp, and various crayfish, and Jack didn't ask for steak once! And although one of our hosts, noticing Jack's difficulty of movement, suggested that his American guest might want to partake of one of Torekov's famous seaweed baths to relieve his back pain, Jack declined, preferring to return that evening to Båstad with me.

South of Båstad, near the town of Lund, there is a famous old castle called Trolleholm. The original structure was built in 1538, and although it's been rebuilt several times over the centuries, it is still an impressive piece of architecture, with its huge central courtyard, surrounded by towers and a moat. Inside, there's a celebrated library which Jack wanted to see, but when I approached the house and explained that I was here with two American friends who would like to tour the interior, I was told that "the Count is not available." I was disappointed, because the current owner, Carl Trolle-Bonde, was a friend of my family. Years later, his daughter, Anna, told me to my great amusement that once her father was informed of who I was with that day, he never forgave himself, and said, "I gave up meeting John F. Kennedy for a siesta!"

But Jack wasn't too disappointed. He said, "All right, let me take a picture of the outside, then. Gunilla, stand over there." He asked Torby for his camera and focused. "No, a little more to the left, so I can get the whole castle and all of you."

But it still wasn't quite right. I was wearing a pair of tortoiseshell sunglasses and had tied a silk Hermes scarf loosely around my neck. "I know how much you love them," he laughed (he'd given them both to me), "but take off the glasses. It's you I want to see!" And he snapped the picture.

～

As a grand finale to the week, I arranged for us to be invited to spend our last night at the home of my old friend Gustav Hagemann, who had a lovely mansion just outside Ystad, on the southern tip of Sweden. Called Ruuthsbo, Gustav's estate was not so far away from Malmö, where the Bulltofta Airport (now called Sturup) was—from which Jack and Torby would depart for France the next morning.

But while planning the end of our week, I became sad, and Jack noticed it. The night before we were due at Gustav's, I became very quiet as Jack and I, along with Torby, headed back to the annex after dinner.

"Is anything wrong?" Jack asked.

"Tomorrow we'll be at Ruuthsbo, with people all around, and then you leave," I said unhappily.

"I love you, Gunilla. I won't really be leaving you."

My temper flared a little bit. "But you *are* leaving, Jack. This has been like a dream, and then . . . what happens? You just disappear and that's it?"

"No, no. I love you, Gunilla. I'll do everything I can to be with you."

"What will you do, Jack?"

"I will talk to my father as soon as I leave here."

The control Joe Kennedy had over Jack's life was becoming more and more clear to me. "Is that the way you live your life? Doing what your father wants you to do? Does your father decide everything?"

"No, Gunilla. Of course not," Jack said quietly.

But he was getting angry, too. "I won't disappear. I promise that. You'll hear from me. Sooner than you think."

Up until then, Torby hadn't said a word, but now he did. We stopped walking for a moment and he turned to me. "He means it, Gunilla," he said sincerely. "Jack will be in touch. You'll see."

I wanted to believe Jack and Torby. And I didn't want anything to spoil the time we had left.

The next afternoon, we set out for Ruuthsbo.

~

Gustav Hagemann has always been one of my closest friends. He always had a great weakness for me, so even though I'd announced that I was coming to visit and bringing "two wonderful American friends with me," I never let on that I was in love with one of them.

Gustav greeted us with open arms and was accommodating and helpful with Jack, who was using his crutches again, but with protestations that it was "just to be safe" and that I should stop worrying about his back.

We all sat down and had some aquavit and talked, and soon several bright and charming friends of Gustav's, as well as his daughter, Lis Stjernsward, who became a famous portrait painter, began to arrive. Then we were all ushered into the dining room, where we were treated to one of the most famous of Sweden's traditional feasts: a crayfish party. Besides the cold crayfish in salt water and dill and a lot of schnapps, there is a cheese called *västerbottencheese,* which is served with toast, and a light meal of filet mignon with vegetables, and for dessert, a light home-baked apple pie with whipped cream. And we sing and say "skoal" all the time. It was really quite festive, especially with the backdrop of Ruuthsbo, with candles flickering against the paneled walls and rows of scenic pictures. I thought it was a lovely but sad ending to such a special and tender week.

But Jack's attentions to me must have been more obviously affectionate than I knew, because over the course of the meal Gustav's manner changed appreciably. I realized by the time dessert was served that the Master of Ruuthsbo had been under the misapprehension all along that I was really coming to visit him, and that my American accomplices were simply along for the ride.

At the end of the evening, our disappointed host, suspecting that Jack and I were together, rose up and, with a fixed smile on his face, said, "Well, Jack, I've enjoyed our conversation. Allow me to show you to your room?"

Jack struggled to his feet and Gustav politely ushered him out. I heard the *clunk, clunk* of his crutches

ascending one flight of steps, then another, and I wondered, Why is Gustav putting Jack up *two flights* to a
guest room on one of the higher floors?

Gustav returned to the sitting room. "My dear," he
said to me, "I'm sure you are very weary after your
drive. Do come with me." He took my hand, and I
thought he was about to lead me to another upstairs
bedroom, but no. To my surprise, he steered me toward a room on the ground floor.

Gustav was really furious with me, but I pretended
not to notice. His plan wasn't a success. When the
house was asleep, I tiptoed upstairs to Jack. His light
was still on, and he was waiting for me.

I fell into his arms and we embraced. Jack Kennedy
made love with a surprising innocence and with all of
his heart. His back troubles might have limited him,
but during our summer week in Sweden, the depth of
our emotions took care of whatever physical limita-
tions Jack had. I was sensitive to his pain, and I could
tell that he was having a particularly bad spell. My
memory returned to the period just after we met, when
I came down with typhoid fever. I remembered how
horribly weak and uncomfortable I had felt, but at
least I recovered. Jack's pain might never go away. I
used every ounce of compassion to comfort him, to
stroke and massage his body where he needed it, to
make sure he felt protected, comfortable, and loved.

He had done this for me, so I did everything I could to show him that I thought he was as beautiful as he made me feel.

That last night was truly wonderful. He said, repeatedly, "I love you, Gunilla. I adore you. I'm crazy about you and I'll do everything I can to be with you." I was completely involved in our intimacy, and I felt the mood was both perfect and fragile. We made love with passion and youthful tenderness.

Later, I pulled the coverlet away, let it fall back over him, stood, and put on my robe and slippers. I walked across the cool painted floorboards and lingered in the doorway for one last look, recalling the touch of his skin, the soft yet strong feel of his lips when we kissed, and his always-tousled hair. I looked at him in the big four-poster bed, then ran back and hugged him one more time. Finally, I rose again to leave.

Before shutting the door, I could just make out his face as his eyes began to close. I left him, and as usual returned to my room.

I woke up early in my bed downstairs, but I stayed there, looking at the ceiling and thinking. I felt a persistent dread because this might be the last time I would see Jack. I knew he'd changed my life. Our need for each other was strong and mutual, but how, where, and when could this continue? Trying to shake away these thoughts, I got up.

By the time I was dressed and went to the breakfast room, Jack and Torby were already there, along with Gustav, who looked first at me, then at the ceiling, then down the hall toward where I had come from. I don't know what he thought, or where he imagined I had spent the night, but he was even-tempered and polite to all of us.

After breakfast, we thanked Gustav for a wonderful time and climbed into the car. This time I drove, because I knew the way to Malmö, outside of which is Bulltofta Airport. I was getting sadder and sadder, but I kept smiling. Jack didn't sing. Torby engaged us all in small talk about our pleasant evening and the charm of Ruuthsbo.

Upon our arrival at Bulltofta, Torby—the perfect comrade and soul of discretion—said, "I'll take our bags and meet you at the gate." He walked off with the suitcases and left us alone for a few minutes. I couldn't help but feel déjà vu; I'd been through something like this before, two years ago in France. But how different this was, really. Piaf's song, *"Je ne regret rien"* passed quickly through my mind.

I kept a cheerful expression pinned onto my face, trying to cover the gnawing heartache I felt inside, willing myself to suppress the tears that were misting my sight. We kissed a long and lingering good-bye. Once again, Jack reached out and pushed the lock of hair off my forehead. Then he cupped the right side of my face with his palm and fingers, holding my cheek in his large hand like a precious treasure. Tearing his gaze away, he looked at his watch and said, "It's time, Gunilla." We went into the terminal.

Inside, Torby and I hugged, and then I put my arms around Jack and held on to him for many moments. Finally we broke our embrace, and they went off to catch their plane. They disappeared through an ordinary door out onto the airfield, and were gone.

I swallowed very hard, but the lump in my throat remained. I didn't stay, or watch them fly away. I drove back to Båstad very fast, and as the miles whipped by, I knew that John Kennedy and I were still unfinished. I could not dismiss the possibility that he would come back into my life, someday, somewhere.

And he did.

HOPE

Back in Båstad, I was withdrawn and immobilized, unable to break through this sudden deep sense of loss. I took long solitary walks through the fields and hills, even occasional quick dips in the bay—the same distractions that had kept me busy while I'd waited nervously for Jack and Torby to arrive just a week or so earlier.

I'm normally a talker, but for two days I was silent. I'm sure Pappa, Ewa, and the rest of our extended family noticed, but it was my compassionate mamma who felt my sadness and tried to comfort me.

After dinner the third night, my mother said, "Gunilla, let's sit on the porch for a while," so I followed her out onto that beautiful, open veranda that made Sjöstugan such a wonderful place to be. I lowered myself stiffly onto a wooden bench, and she sat in a cane rocking chair, not speaking a word at first, just looking down at the water as dusk fell. I wondered what was next. Mamma and I had often had mother/daughter "heart-to-heart" talks, and I felt one was coming.

Finally, she turned to me with a half-smile. "Do you miss him?" she asked.

"Yes."

"I know that you love him, Gunilla." She turned back to the view. "He feels the same way."

My heart leapt. I tried not to show it. But Mamma looked at me, and even in the fading light, she could see the flush on my face. "How . . . how do you . . ." I stammered.

"You know we talked while he was here."

"Yes, but he wouldn't tell me anything about it."

"Of course not. He's not happy with his marriage, but I think that was clear to all of us."

I drew myself up a bit, trying to be brave and courageous. "Will he divorce her?" I asked, in much too small a voice.

"Ahhh. That you should ask. Jack has great charm. As you well know. It's a gift. He charms me every time we talk."

She wasn't answering my question. "And? Yes? What, Mamma?"

"He says he wants to leave her and marry you."

"Oh!" I said.

"But . . ." Her voice lowered and she turned to me. She patted my leg and said, "Gunilla, dear, try to be re-alistic. The situation is not easy, and you know it."

"But why? If he loves me . . ."

"Oh, he may indeed love you. But remember what Eric said? Our Jack wants to be the president of the

United States someday, and his father wants that for him, too. Do you really suppose he would divorce Jackie now? For a Swedish girl nobody in his country has ever heard of?"

I didn't—couldn't—answer. I had the sudden if immature thought that I was just as acceptable as Miss Bouvier had been. I felt like stamping my foot and shouting out a list: I was not an American girl, true, but I came from a fine old family. I'd been presented at the Swedish Court by Gertrud Bostrom, whose husband, Wolmar, had been our ambassador to Washington. I had danced in the ballrooms of palaces with portraits of my own ancestors on the walls. I'd been on the covers of several national magazines. Only three Decembers ago, when I was studying at Hasselbaken's Hotel School, I'd been chosen to be Santa Lucia for the annual Lucia festival, and I'd carried it off, candles on my head and all. I'd done my duty, and nobody knew I was scared to death. I really could *perform* when I had to.

So what was wrong with me? The answer was silently but firmly: "Nothing at all!" Besides, I kept repeating to myself deep within, *If he loves me, if he loves me and doesn't love her . . .*

I sighed. No use saying anything out loud, especially anything like that, because then I would have to endure another of Mamma's commonsense speeches about using my head over my heart, and I didn't need to hear it again. So I just looked down at my fingers, tracing the pattern on my skirt back and forth, up and down. I must have looked crushed.

My mother realized she had sounded harsher than she meant to. "I'm fond of him, too," she said. "Don't misunderstand. I think his affection for you is real, and I think in his heart he would like his marriage to somehow disappear. When he said, 'In a different world, I would ask you and Pappa Olle for Gunilla's hand,' he meant it. But I had to ask him, 'Jack, what about this world? The one we really live in now?'"

"Did he say anything, Mamma?"

"He said, 'This world, this path I'm on—my family, my country—this is difficult. I don't know how to answer you, Brita, but I want to remind you that I love your daughter.' So I let it go. I can't force Jack to do anything. And I can't force you to feel anything less than you do."

She looked at me for a moment, and I saw a sympathetic smile flicker across her face. My mother was very emotional, but she didn't like to show it, so she rose, slowly, in her majestic way. The session was over. "Now then, let's go inside before it gets too dark. You could start your packing. You're leaving the day after tomorrow, you know."

"I know." We went back into the house.

~

Only twenty-four hours after our return from Båstad to Stockholm, a letter arrived from the Hotel du Cap d'Antibes on the Côte d'Azur, postmarked August 22, 1955. Still aglow with the memories and emotions of my romantic week, I tore it open more eagerly than ever before.

The greeting was "Dearest Gunilla." This was new—more tender and intimate than before. I felt like kissing the paper. The letter was wistful, yearning. He asked how I had survived our day at "the farm," which is what he insisted upon calling Ruuthsbo. He worried that I hadn't seemed sad enough when I said good-bye to him and Torby at the airport, and asked if I had been relieved to see them go. Relieved? I was in despair. Apparently, my pretense at bravery and calm had been an even better act than I thought. The truth was that I had felt as if my heart were being ripped out, but I didn't want to show it.

Then he wrote that he'd just learned that his wife and sister-in-law were arriving at Cap d'Antibes any moment, and that his feelings were now complicated, after our week together, "my Swedish flicka." But my tears truly began to spill over when I read that he had been unable to do much else except sit in the warmth of the sun, stare out over the sea, "and think of Gunilla . . ."

He did love me. I wanted to run to my mother's room and show her the letter, but I resisted the impulse. Somehow, keeping it to myself made it mine and more real. And, "All love, Jack," at the bottom made it even more meaningful.

Jack called from the Riviera. I wasn't home, but my mother said he was happy to speak to her, and did so for a long time. Once again, I had to force the information out of her, but this time she ended up being at least a little more forthcoming:

"He says he is just biding his time, thinking about you, and waiting for his wife and sister-in-law to leave Cap d'Antibes."

"And then what?"

Mamma hesitated, and then looked resigned. "When they've gone, he's going to stop over at Capri. He wants you to join him there."

My mother's expression made my smile disappear. "You don't think I should go, do you?" I said softly.

"I know I told you a year ago that you were an adult and had to make up your own mind. But, Gunilla, I can't watch you set yourself up for a broken heart."

"What did you tell Jack?" I asked.

"I simply reminded him that he is a married man."

"I thought you said we were all aware of that, Mother!" I was getting angry, which was something I rarely did in Mamma's presence.

"We are aware of it. I wanted to make sure Mr. Kennedy is also aware of it."

~

Jack stopped calling for a while, I guessed because he was waiting for his wife and sister-in-law to leave before resuming his pursuit. But I couldn't be sure, because we all took a long weekend trip to Rockelstad Castle, about two and a half hours outside of Stockholm. Now owned by my distant cousin Christer von Post, Rockelstad is important historically to Sweden. In the 1920s, the castle was home to Baron Eric von Rosen and he had quite an interesting visitor: a young, handsome, and ambitious German named Hermann Göring, whose career in the military was already on the ascendant. During his stay, Göring fell in love with a beautiful young girl, Carin Kantzow, born Baroness Fock, who was the sister of Eric's wife, Mary. My father—in fact, my whole family—believed that Hitler was a madman from the very beginning. Still, many Swedish people, including those who remained violently anti-Nazi, had to admit that the affection

Göring felt for our country—and his beloved Carin (who died at thirty-three of cancer, and for whom Göring built a house outside Berlin called Carin-hall)—may have been one reason we were spared during the war. This is pehaps the only nice thing any of us have to say about a member of the Nazi Party, let alone a man who became one of Hitler's chief lieu-tenants.

That weekend, while enjoying the pleasures of Rockelstad and the cool, clear early-autumn days and nights, I kept wondering if the telephone was ringing in our apartment back in Stockholm. There would be no one there to take the call.

My wondering stopped when we returned home. A telegram was waiting. Jack desperately needed to talk to me, and asked me to wire him at the Hotel Qui-sisana in Capri, and asked where he could contact me. It was signed "Miss you. Love—Jack."

I cabled him that afternoon, and the next morning the telephone rang early.

"It's so beautiful here," he said. "It would be even more beautiful if you could come down."

"Oh, Jack, I do miss you."

"I don't just miss you. I need you. I feel alive when we're together, and I don't want to give that up. Gu-nilla, please come."

"Jack, I just . . . I don't know . . ." I was thinking

about his wife, and I was nervous. It was one thing for Mamma to report her conversations with him on that touchy subject, but in two years Jack and I had never even brought it up. A rush of emotion swept through me. In my mind, I was suddenly back in Jack's room at Ruuthsbo and I could again touch him, hear him whisper, "I love you, Gunilla. I adore you. I'm crazy about you and I'll do anything I can to be with you."

I spoke into the receiver. "Yes. I remember how we were. I remember too much sometimes."

His voice was soft. "I wish I had even one of your photographs with me. Torby hasn't sent me the one I took at the castle yet, so the only way for me to see you is if you come down to Capri. Please, do come, Gunilla."

What to do? What to say? As always, my heart was in total conflict with my head.

Too long a silence. I swallowed hard and took a deep breath. "Jack, I don't feel it's right just after your family has left. Båstad was beautiful, and I'll never forget that week, but . . ." Why couldn't I say it?

"All right. But what?"

I just blurted it out. "You're married!"

Very slowly and steadily, he said, "Gunilla, I've been married for two years. What's changed?"

"Me. Maybe I've changed."

"How?"

"Maybe I'm in love with you now."

Suddenly, I thought we'd lost our connection. "Jack? Jack, are you there?"

"Yes. Gunilla, I . . . Please don't get angry at me again, but I have to talk to my father about us."

I certainly didn't want another argument. I was hopelessly in love.

I said, "All right."

~

There were two more calls, during which any discussion of his marriage was avoided. But Jack begged me again to make the trip to Capri. I said no. Some voice inside kept repeating, *If he means what he says, he'll have to find a way to come to you, or at least meet halfway.* It was a voice I'd heard before. It was the same instinct that had urged me a year and a half before not to go to Paris, or the South of France, or to America. *A man chases a girl until she catches him.*

So Jack switched tactics.

From then on, the only mention of his Capri invitation was a color postcard of the Piccola Marina ("the little beach"). On the back, he wrote, "I wish *you* could have been here." Subject closed.

I knew I was right not to have gone, but I also yearned to be with him again. As before, I dreamed of what it could have been like, lying in the sun with him, sailing with him, loving him. Just looking into his eyes, seeing the hurt and happiness I knew was there, behind their clear, sometimes blazing blueness. I remembered—no, I could actually see this as I sat in our living room at Styrmansgatan—the tenderness in his gaze; the little boy he had been, so riddled with physical pain and emotional need, so desperate to please, and the man who couldn't hide the disappointment of his marriage.

And listening to him, or even better, being listened to, would have been a thrill. The fact that Jack was the first person I'd ever met who made me feel important, made me feel that what I said mattered, was just as powerful an attraction as the romantic pull of his fascinating personality. At each and every turn during our week together, Jack wanted to know what *I* thought about the events of the day. And with Jack, there was never a dull moment.

It would have been marvelous to be with him again, for many reasons. In Capri, or anywhere. But I had purposely shut that little Italian window of opportunity. Now Jack began to talk about the rest of his European itinerary. "I have to be in Poland next week," he said on the phone. "I'm going to look up your cousin." That pleased me. I knew how much Eric and his wife and children had enjoyed Jack's company in Båstad.

Meanwhile, the social season in Stockholm was warming up again, as the temperature cooled. Hostesses all over town, including at Drottningholm, where the King's palace sprawled across acres of manicured grounds and lakes, invited me to parties. And I visited old friends of my family at some of the great houses outside the city—Pelle and Lott von Essen at their magnificent castle in Uppland, called Salsta, and especially Hubbe and Muj von Schinkel, who lived at Tido, in Västmanland; their dinner dances were in the old style, like eighteenth-century balls, and lasted until two or three in the morning.

I was considered a very eligible young woman, and everyone was eager to introduce me to similarly eligible men. Although I met several, a part of me was always with my American senator. I was an all-or-nothing woman, and I still am.

I didn't hear from Jack Kennedy until he got to Poland. I was beginning to feel a peculiar tension between my love for him and always needing to wait for his calls. Yes, I could write to him, or wire him if he gave me an address, but that wasn't good enough. My hope was beginning to fade.

I'd not brought up my frustration about this before, because I feared his response would have something to do with Jacqueline. I meant to confront him with this the next time he called. And he did, from the American embassy, on the second day after his arrival in Warsaw.

"Gunilla? How have you been?" His voice was tender and sincere.

"I've been all right, Jack," I said. "How was your trip?"

"Pretty rocky. I got here in an old American DC-3 flown by a Polish crew. I don't think they knew that plane very well! But we made it. I went over to the old ghetto yesterday. It's depressing. But I'd rather talk about you. What have you been up to?"

"I've been riding, and I've been out a lot, to nice dinners and dances. But I miss you, darling."

"Me, too. I often think about our week together."

"So do I." I wondered if he'd contacted my cousin Eric, who was now back at the Swedish embassy in Warsaw. "Did you talk to Eric, Jack?"

"Yes. Yesterday. I told him everything. I mean, about how I feel, about my life at home. I still want to be with you. I'm going to do it. I'm going to telephone my father this afternoon."

My heart raced. He promised to call me that night

to report on his conversation with old Joe. He finished by saying, "I love you, Gunilla. You will be home when I call?"

"I love you, too. I'll be there."

~

While my parents and Ewa went to a dinner party, I chose to stay at home, saying I was tired. But I was restless and nervous, waiting for Jack's call. I picked up magazines and put them down. I walked from room to room. I rearranged flowers. I smoked a cigarette. I walked back and forth. I smoked another cigarette. Finally, the phone rang. It was late, but my mother, father, and sister were still out.

I ran into the drawing room and answered.

"Gunilla?"

"Yes, Jack."

"I talked to my father."

I did a slow-breathing exercise to calm down.

"It wasn't a very pleasant conversation," he said.

"What happened?"

"You don't know him. But he can be—he's very harsh."

I waited for more. Now I was impatient, and I desperately needed an explanation. "Jack, please tell me what he said. What you both said. I need to know."

"I—I told him about you. I'm sorry, but—apart

from your family, and your friends in Båstad—I've never talked about you to anybody except Torby. It was so hard, Gunilla. It's impossible to bring up my troubles with my wife to him. He doesn't even want to hear about it, because she likes him and he responds to that."

"But you told him about me?"

"I said that I'd fallen in love with you, and I didn't think I could go on the way things are now. That I wanted to end my marriage so that I could be with you."

"What did he say?"

"He didn't just say it. He yelled at me, 'You're out of your mind. You're going to be president someday. This would ruin everything. Divorce is impossible. Look at what happened with me and Gloria Swanson!' He also said that whether I had a happy marriage or not wasn't the point. He repeated something he's been telling us all our lives. He said, 'Can't you get it into your head that it's not important what you really are? The only important thing is what people *think* you are!' "

My heart was sinking. "Oh, Jack, I don't know. This is getting complicated."

"I know. It sounds that way. Look. I feel terrible. I can't stand talking about this—talking about us—without being near you. I'm going to think of something. I have a meeting early tomorrow, but I can telephone you around lunchtime. A little before or after. Please wait for me. Can you?"

"Yes. Call me here tomorrow."

And so again I waited. The next day, Jack called before noon. He sounded eager and expectant. My spirits rose.

"I have an idea," he said, almost breathlessly. "Is it so hard for you to come to Copenhagen?"

"No." I knew I could manage that no matter how much Mamma wouldn't want me to go.

"I have to be in Zurich for two days, then back to Warsaw, then home. But I'll have the embassy book me through to Copenhagen. If I can work it out, can you meet me there? It will be within this week."

"Yes. I can come. I would love to see you, too."

There was a slight sigh of relief on the phone, almost imperceptible, but there. "I'll let you know as soon as I can. Oh—and, Gunilla? Remember—I love you."

"I love you, too."

~

"I'm afraid the Copenhagen trip is going to be difficult," Jack said during his next call.

Before I could express my disappointment, his voice brightened. "But I have another idea. Why don't you come over to the States for a visit?"

Jack had caught me at a very vulnerable moment. The night before, I'd been to a medium-sized party. The host was one of my parents' great friends, so I had to attend. With a half-heart, I'd pulled out a nice evening dress and a pair of good shoes, and embarked like a reluctant Cinderella on her way to the ball, knowing certainly that my prince would not be there. He wasn't.

My social life since Jack left had been just as I had reported to him—riding, and "nice dinners and dances"—but although many of the people I met were attractive, some were also dull. I really didn't even want to pretend interest if a man started to talk to me about his family or his stables, but I had been bred to have manners at all times, so I would smile, nodding sweetly every now and then. Trying to conceal my boredom, I would just continue to dance. I missed the kind of attention Jack paid to me, and his genuine concern for what I had to say.

My longing for him had become more intense than ever, and all I could do to stay sane was to think about his charm, his wonderful face, his humor. Jack Kennedy had opened up a whole new world to me.

So the idea of visiting him in the States, even for a short time, was more than attractive. If we couldn't meet in Copenhagen, then a vacation for a week or so in America—especially if I could spend time with him—was irresistible. I'm afraid I answered "Yes!" much too quickly and emotionally, because, as always, my heart jumped in where a sounder mind should have prevailed.

While I waited for further word, in desperation, I called my cousin Eric in Warsaw and asked him, "Did John Kennedy discuss me with you?"

Eric answered, "Yes."

"Did he tell you he loved me and wanted to leave his wife?"

"Gunilla, I am going to answer you truthfully this one time, and while I am alive, it will remain between the two of us. Yes, he did tell me that. But I want you to know here and now that if it arises again, my answer will always be 'No comment.'"

Eric kept his word. Until the day he died, if any discussion of the nature of my relationship with Jack Kennedy ever came up, he refused to either deny or confirm anything. He would just say, "No comment."

Although I didn't really need Eric's confirmation, his words reinforced my belief that for whatever it was worth—for now or forever—Jack and I loved each other, and that wasn't going to disappear, no matter what.

~

Another letter from Jack, postmarked in Zurich but written at the airport in Poland, arrived only days after we spoke. Since Copenhagen proved to be impossible, he pleaded once again with me to come to the States.

I was struck not only by his need for me, despite the complications that kept arising to keep us apart, but also, this letter actually *looked* different from the others. Before, when he had written from Washington, even from the hospital when he was suffering so much, his handwriting was large, generous, and with an up-sweep that looked confident and happy. But now his penmanship was smaller, measured, and was written across the page in straight lines.

The way Jack's pen formed his words revealed his emotions. I held the paper in my hands, and realized that he and I were feeling the same sadness. Copenhagen wasn't going to work out.

So. No Copenhagen. Capri was finished, by my own hand. The obstructions were enormous: Jack's marriage; his father's hold on him; his political ambitions. The thought of rushing off to America and falling into his arms was exciting, a wild dream. But I knew that the wise thing for me to do was to end it and once and for all get on with my life.

ANDERS

Jack called in early October, a week before his scheduled departure for Washington. We had the longest telephone conversation yet. His plans for us had developed into something far beyond a casual visit; he wanted much more of a commitment.

"I can arrange for you to come to New York," he said. "Once you're there, I'll take care of you. I can put you up at the Carlyle for a while until we decide what's next."

"What will be next, Jack?"

He'd obviously been thinking about it, because he didn't hesitate at all before saying, "I will make you a top model in New York. I can introduce you to the right people. Of course, you'd have to lose a few pounds. American models are skinny, and you look, well, maybe too healthy!"

"You know how I like good food."

His laugh again. That wonderful sound. "I do. Don't worry. We won't want you *too* thin."

"And how will I fit into your life, Jack?"

"I love you. You will see. I will find a way."

I wanted to tell him how I thought of him with

such love each day, and how at night, my last thoughts before drifting off to sleep were of him.

But I just asked, "When?"

"Tomorrow. The day after. Next week. I have to see you," he said urgently.

"I'll let you know."

"Soon? Please, Gunilla? Write me at—"

"I know. At the Senate Office Building."

But I didn't. It was hard enough for me to express myself in Swedish, but as I thought and thought, I realized my feelings about taking such a dramatic step were much too complex, nearly impossible for me to relate in any language, let alone writing them down in English. I still wanted Jack as much as he wanted me, but to journey across the Atlantic to America to see him again without knowing for how long, without knowing whether he would ever be free, without knowing very much about New York, or the United States, for that matter—these were all added obstacles to the romantic dream I had about the two of us.

But I had learned by now that obstacles were put in our paths to be overcome, and I knew I was daring enough to fight through them. I felt adventurous and strong, and I was still wildly in love.

I went to the American embassy in Stockholm to inquire about getting a visa, and because I was acquainted with a woman named Olga Tyszkiewicz, I contacted her brother, Serge Obolensky, in New York. Serge was a tall Russian émigré whose pedigree, bearing, and aristocratic charm had made him a major presence in American society. He was officially a "public relations executive," but he was always perceived as much more than that. His major client was New York's Ambassador Hotel on Park Avenue, and when I informed him that I might be coming over to New York and might need some work while I was there, he suggested that he could try to arrange a job for me at the hotel's reception desk. This was reassuring, just in case I needed it.

After two days and two fitful nights, I made a decision. I placed a transatlantic call to the Senate in Washington, D.C., and left a message for Senator Kennedy to call me as soon as he could, and I didn't care whether he was annoyed or not.

He wasn't annoyed at all. He called back the following day. The only problem was that instead of me, he got my mother, and I returned to the apartment just as she was hanging up. I asked her who was calling, and she told me. The look on her face was that of a loving but fierce tigress protecting her young.

I said I was going to America to see him.

"Gunilla, let's talk about this, dear."

She got up and walked slowly across the Persian carpet, toward a pale gold silk-cushioned eighteenth-

century *canapé* placed against one of the wide case-
ment windows overlooking Styrmansgatan. Now she
sat upon it, straightened her skirt, and looked at me.

I sat down opposite her. I could see the tips of bare
treetops outside. My back was warmed by a classic
porcelain stove in the corner, but both my mother and
the autumn tableau behind her had the look of an early
frost.

"As always, Jack and I had a long talk," she said
evenly.

"What did he say?"

"Let's start with his idea of turning you into a
model and putting you up in a New York hotel."

"All right. I'm sure you had an opinion about
that."

"Indeed. I said, 'We love you, Jack, but this is not
for Gunilla.'"

I felt tears well up inside. I think I understood. But I
needed to talk to him. "I've got to speak to him myself."

Mamma stared directly at me. "I know. I didn't
even have to suggest that. He'll be tied up for a few
weeks, but as soon as he can, he said he will talk with
you."

"Will he?"

"Jack and I have a more-than-cordial relationship.
We understand each other. His promise is good. He'll

call. I know that. There is something he must talk to you about."

"What?"

"He will tell it to you on the phone."

~

The summer before I met Jack, I had trained in Stockholm as a laboratory assistant. Now this experience came in handy. I wanted to be kept busy, so I volunteered for work doing research with the doctors and professors at Södersjukhuset Hospital. I was particularly interested in antibacterial hygiene. I felt useful, engaged in a job that could help and protect people as well.

I kept up my social life, too. I accepted an invitation to another of those large, gracious parties that my friends Curt—known as "Curre"—Smith and his wife, Sonia, liked to give at Värsta Gård, their mansion outside of Stockholm. When I arrived at the party that night, Curre immediately led me over to a tall, handsome, and athletic-looking man in an impeccable suit.

"Gunilla, this is Anders Ekman," he said, with a tone of conspiracy and triumph. "*He* is the man for you!" Curre then turned to Anders and said, "This, Anders, is the girl for you."

I had to admit that he cut a very appealing figure: strong, healthy-looking, with just the kind of smile I liked—real and unpretentious. After exchanging names, I moved to my table, but when dinner was over and the music started to play, he was the only man in the room I didn't dance with. When I left, Mr. Ekman was looking at me with a great deal of interest.

I found out a few weeks later that Anders Ekman was estranged from his wife and that the divorce papers were about to be signed.

I fully intended to continue playing my belle-of-the-ball role that season, except that a kind of exhaustion had crept up upon me and taken hold. My heart muscle was still damaged from the typhoid fever, so every now and then I felt weak. I knew enough to take it easy when that happened.

One Sunday evening in October, I had dinner with my family and planned to go to sleep early. I was tired after a late Saturday night at yet another dinner dance. I'd washed my hair and was on my way to bed, when I heard the telephone ring. A minute later my mother called to say it was for me.

I put on my robe and hurried down the hall. The eager expression on my face was a clear sign to Mamma that I hoped it was Jack. But she shook her head. "It's Curre Smith," she said.

Curre sounded energetic and enthusiastic. "Gunilla, dear, you must come and join us. We're at Cecil's with Genia and Gregor, and guess who else?"

I really didn't care much, but I feigned interest. "I don't know. Who?"

"I have your future husband here. Anders Ekman!"

Anders Ekman again. Perhaps I should take another look at him, I thought. I rallied my strength. "I've eaten already, but I'll come over for a drink, or dessert and coffee," I told Curre.

The Restaurant Cecil was elegant, with a fashionable clientele, so I wasn't going to wear just anything. I brushed my hair and put on a chic purple suit and a red shawl, and wore a gold chain around my neck. In my cashmere coat, I was ready.

I love nightspots, especially lively ones with happy people, good food and service, and an attractive decor. Cecil was really a bar/restaurant, very much like the Hotel Carlyle in New York is today, with piano music, comfortable furniture in the 1930s style, and the most amusing customers in town. It was especially popular as a meeting place on Saturday afternoons, when we'd go in and order cocktails and hors d'oeuvres and exchange the news of the day. On that night Curre called, I arrived at Cecil, sat down in one of the big, luxurious chairs, and was reacquainted with Anders Ekman. Within a half hour, something started to happen between us.

Like John Kennedy, this man was actually paying attention to what I thought and said. He was really

very handsome, and there was a comfortable and secure aspect to him that drew me in. Also, of course, he
was Swedish, so our conversation had the added ease
of a shared native tongue.

When Anders drove me home, he asked if he could
take me to dinner the following week, and I accepted.

Back in the apartment, I knocked on the door of
my sister's room, then went in and sat down on her
bed.

"Ewa. I think I've met a nice man. His name is Anders Ekman."

"My goodness, 'Nilla! Every woman in Stockholm
is after him!"

I didn't know that, but I wasn't surprised. I thought
it was because he was so good-looking. But his popu-
larity didn't matter to me. If I found Anders attractive,
it was because I simply felt that he was. As with Jack,
the only thing that was interesting to me was the man
himself.

"Could he make you forget Jack?" Ewa asked me.

"I can never forget Jack."

If Jack's strong hold on my heart wasn't loosened
by Anders, it was only because they were so different.
Jack burned like a brilliant comet in the sky. Anders
was like the rich soil of earth. Quieter. Solid and
strong, a rock.

After two more dinners, I realized that Anders's

preoccupations were not close to mine, but he engaged my interest. He was a landowner and sportsman who liked fishing and rising at dawn for shooting, and hunting and tennis at his place "in the north," a house called Tjälls Gård, more than three hundred miles above Stockholm—which was pretty far north. I assumed it was a hunting lodge tucked into the woods and didn't ask much more about it.

Every day, I waited for a phone call from America, but a new understanding was nudging at me: If I could never have Jack in the way I needed and wanted him, perhaps Anders could offer me a happy life.

We had a third date, during which he assured me that he and his wife, Mimmi, were through. She would be signing the final decree any day. But then he announced that he was going off to Holland to visit Louise, an old love he knew there, and would return in a week. I knew that this woman had been Anders's first love, long before he met Mimmi, but I had a surprising reaction: I was not jealous. Ewa asked me why.

"You can't heat up old porridge," I answered.

This was a self-assurance that was new for me, and I attributed it to Jack. If a man as wonderful as John Kennedy could fall in love with me, then I allowed myself a growing confidence: Anders's old girlfriend was not a threat.

I was right about the old porridge. When he returned from Holland, Anders was more romantic than ever. He took me out for an evening at the Grand Hotel. He was a wonderful dancer, attentive and graceful. I looked forward to seeing him more and more.

~

And then, just as he had promised Mamma he would, Jack called. "I'm sorry it's been so long, Gunilla. There's been so much going on here. There's talk of my running for vice president next year. A man named Stevenson will probably be up for president. I'm not sure. I think it's a long shot. But you don't care about that. How have you been?"

I wasn't entirely unaware of Jack's political aspirations. Every few weeks I stopped by the Grand Hotel and headed for the big international newsstand there. Even finding myself in the heart of Stockholm, I was reminded of Jack, remembering what he'd said in his long letter from the hospital in New York that past December. Besides lifting my heart, writing that I had "a beautiful, controlled face" that still haunted him— a sentence that still haunted me—he'd mentioned a nurse on his floor from Sweden. But he complained that she was dark and had black hair. He had asked her why she'd left "the Venice of the North" for New York, and she'd replied that Manhattan was much nicer. He seemed astonished by this, concluding that she was probably French. I got the impression he didn't care for her much.

I thought of that letter often. It was not only romantic and moving, but he was right about Stockholm, which is built on more than a dozen islands and is indeed like Venice. But I also wondered about this dark-haired Swedish nurse. Despite my desire to stop obsessing about such things, I couldn't help speculating if she was anything like his dark-haired wife of French descent.

So although I knew it wasn't contributing to my mental and emotional health, I often bought the Paris edition of the *Herald Tribune,* and a couple of American magazines—*Time* and *Newsweek*—at the Grand Hotel. Now and then, sometimes buried in the back pages, sometimes more visible, there were items about John F. Kennedy, but reading about him only upset me. The most significant news item, as far as I was concerned, had been a short paragraph in one of the columns reporting that the young Senator Kennedy and his lovely wife, Jacqueline, had bought a large Georgian mansion called Hickory Hill in Virginia. There were stables for her horses and a pool for him to exercise his bad back. Jackie was redecorating the entire house.

Now I trembled at his voice on the phone. But I tried to sound tranquil. I did care about his career, and even more about how he was feeling. I answered his question. "I've been fine, Jack. Very busy. Your life must be quite exciting right now." I was silent for just a moment, and he was, too.

Then he said, "I wanted to call you even sooner. Every day I thought about it. Gunilla, I'm so—I'm so sorry, and so sad. I just can't—I mean, I have to follow this course. It's as though everything here is rolling along without any brakes. I can't stop it."

I wondered if he meant *can't* or *won't*. "Do you want to be vice president?" I asked him.

"Honestly? I don't think I'll get it. I think I should wait for the big one, the big job, in four years. There's a slim chance at that, if everything falls in place."

This was all important. Important to Jack's political future and perhaps to the future of his country. It was also important to us, and to my future.

"Jack, my mother said you had to tell me something."

"Yes." His voice sounded choked. "Yes, I do have to tell you something." This time the pause seemed endless. And I wasn't going to break it.

He said, "Jackie is pregnant."

I was stunned.

"Gunilla? Are you all right, dear?"

"No, I'm not. My dear Jack, we won't ever see each other again now, will we?"

"Don't think that."

Suddenly, I had a lot to say. "What else can I think? You can't leave your wife now. You can't leave your career. I've been living in a sort of dream. I love you, Jack, I always will, and I was tempted to come to New York, I really was, but I have to have a life, and a future. I want my own family."

He took his time before he said, "I do, too. I hope a baby will help. But I can't feel about my wife the way I do about you."

"Yes you can! Try! I think she's trying very hard!" I took a deep breath and said slowly, "I've met a very nice man here. I'm interested in him. I think he would make a wonderful husband."

After a short pause, he said, "I'm happy for you. You're right. About everything. I'm being selfish."

"No, you're just being—"

"Selfish. Because I wasn't thinking enough about you. Only about me. Do me a favor, Gunilla, will you?"

"Of course."

"Let me know what you decide to do."

"I'll tell you . . . whatever happens. And you know I wish you all the best things in the world."

"Thank you. I love you, my dear."

I sat by the telephone for a very long time.

R E U N I O N

During that autumn of 1955, I took a pre-Christmas job for the second year selling accessories at Nordiska Kompaniet, Stockholm's Saks Fifth Avenue, work I enjoyed and did well. I also graduated with flying colors from Angeldorff's cooking school. And I continued to see a great deal of Anders Ekman. Toward the beginning of December, he said he wanted to speak to my mother and father.

"He wishes to ask for your hand in marriage," Mamma reported. "Of course, we like him, Gunilla, but I said, 'Don't you think you should ask her first? We already approve of you, Anders.'"

He did, I said yes, and the ring was on my finger. I was engaged.

Soon after that, Anders invited me and my parents to spend New Year's up at Tjälls Gård, and we accepted.

On December 30, Mamma, Pappa, and I took the night train up north. It was still dark when Anders met us at the Långsele station in a big Mercedes. He drove for several miles and then pulled into a private road and said, "We're here," but I didn't see anything. All the headlights showed were snow-covered foliage and fields. It turned out that "here" meant that all the miles and miles of forest and farmland around us belonged to him. And then we spun around a corner, the trees disappeared, and a nineteenth-century manor house with most of the windows lit up like a Christmas tree loomed before us.

"There's Tjäll," Anders said as we drew closer.

Tearing our astonished eyes away from the Palladian-like formality of this mansion, with the stately lines and simple geometry that are typical of the Swedish country style, but with a strong French influence, my mother and I shared a glance. So *this* was his little hunting lodge in the woods!

Two liveried servants appeared instantly and unpacked the trunk. We entered. The main house at Tjälls Gård had twenty-four rooms, a built-in pool, and was surrounded by tennis courts, vegetable and flower gardens, and carefully tended grounds. As we were shown to our quarters to freshen up and change for breakfast, I began to realize that even if Anders was one of the wealthiest men in Scandinavia after all, it wasn't what intrigued me. My affection for him had already begun to ripen long before this visit. The sorrowful void left by Jack was slowly being filled with another kind of devotion, and I welcomed it with relief and open arms.

~

New Year's Eve was a classic holiday, straight out of *Doctor Zhivago,* with sleighbells ringing as we sped through the snowdrifts to Multra church, roaring open fires, candlelight, and festive Swedish meals. We made up for the cold and the long, dark nights of winter by eating heartily. There were several different kinds of terrines, whitefish, large baked hams accompanied by dark bread to dip in the juice, meatballs, herring, sausage, and apple strudel. Anders was particularly fond of pig's feet, but I was definitely not; I couldn't stand to look at them! There was singing, dancing, plentiful spirits, good fine wines, and lots of laughter.

We followed an age-old Swedish New Year's Eve tradition: Just before the stroke of midnight, as the churchbells began to ring outside, we turned on the radio to listen to a popular old actor named Anders de Wahl give his yearly reading of "Ring Klocka, Ring!" and then, when the clocks reached midnight, we threw open all the doors of the house to welcome 1956 and broke out the champagne.

After a happily exhausted stay, we were back in Stockholm a little more than a week later.

The remainder of the von Post/Ekman courtship was an exciting whirlwind. Anders's energy was phenomenal, but I hung in. Unfortunately, upon hearing of our engagement, his estranged wife, Mimmi, refused to

sign the final papers. In January, Anders told me he was
going on safari in Africa and asked me to accompany
him. I said, "No, dear. We're engaged and you aren't
divorced yet. I don't think it's right." So I left Stockholm and went to Vienna to study German and read
Goethe, lodging with a nice family named von Schoen-
burg, who lived at Rainergasse 11.

Three weeks later a telegram arrived from Africa.
Mimmi was going to sign the papers after all.

> WAITING FOR YOU IN NAIROBI.
> LOVE YOU. PLEASE COME. TICKET
> ARRANGED. LOVE ANDERS.

So I went. Sightseeing, hunting, a photo safari. I
even rode in competition with Gustaf Kleen, who
everybody called Romulus because he was born in
Rome. He was the nephew of Karen Blixen, better
known as the writer Isak Dinesen. Anders and I were
planning to be married in Nairobi, but Mimmi still
didn't sign.

We sailed back through the Suez Canal, from
Mombasa to Marseilles, and then traveled up to Paris.
I began to see that Mr. Ekman's energy was going to be
hard to match. But I like energetic, vital men, so I kept
up, and took naps whenever I could.

While we were in Paris, I saw that the Paris edition

Top: Pappa Olle.

Above: Brita, my mother, when I was four months old. Note the Napoleonic curl, the reason Pappa nicknamed me Napoleona.

Right: With Ewa, my younger sister.

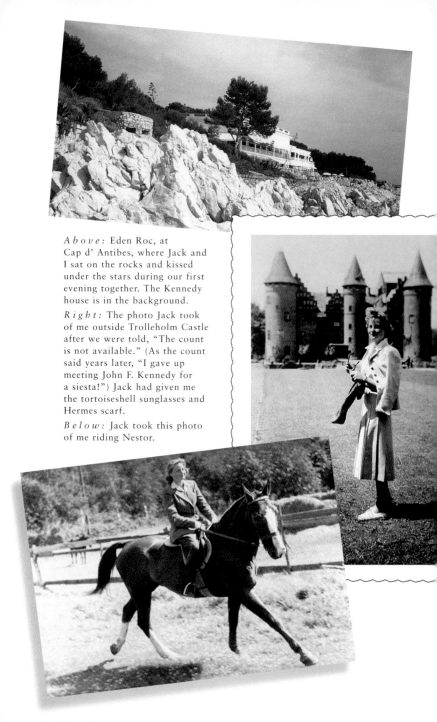

A b o v e : Eden Roc, at Cap d' Antibes, where Jack and I sat on the rocks and kissed under the stars during our first evening together. The Kennedy house is in the background.

R i g h t : The photo Jack took of me outside Trolleholm Castle after we were told, "The count is not available." (As the count said years later, "I gave up meeting John F. Kennedy for a siesta!") Jack had given me the tortoiseshell sunglasses and Hermes scarf.

B e l o w : Jack took this photo of me riding Nestor.

Right: Tjälls Gård, Anders Ekman's "hunting lodge"—with 24 rooms, a built-in pool, and tennis courts.

Below: Tending one of the flower gardens outside Tjäll.

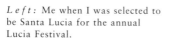

Left: Me when I was selected to be Santa Lucia for the annual Lucia Festival.

Below: Jack and Jackie cutting the cake at their wedding, his brother Bobby watching.

Left: Dining with Anders during our courtship.

Below: Our wedding photo. Anders had threatened to find the fictional hairdresser who'd curled my hair and "punch him in the nose."

Left: In Africa, 1956.

Below: Anders with our oldest daughter, Andrea, 1959.

Bottom: Anders with his plane, a few days before he died.

A b o v e : My sister
Ewa, left, and me
with the former Dutch
Ambassador Jan
Visser.

R i g h t : My son Ian,
who died at seven
months, here at four
months.

Left: With Wisner in Greenwich, 1970.

Below: With Gustav Hagemann, in his eighties, taken ten years ago.

Bottom: Ruuthsbo, Gustav Hagemann's house, where Jack and I spent our last night together.

of the *Herald Tribune* reported that John Kennedy might make a serious bid for the vice presidency during the Democratic Convention. There was a photograph of him. I clipped it out and put it in my handbag. My pleasure and sense of ease with Anders was deepening, but Jack still held on to a significant piece of my heart. I would save many other pictures of Jack as the years lengthened.

In another edition of the same paper, I read that Jacqueline had miscarried. I wished I could have done something to comfort Jack. This was the first time I'd mentioned Jack to Anders. I said, "I met John Kennedy on the Riviera a few years ago, and I feel sad that he and his wife have lost a baby."

When we arrived back in Stockholm, Mimmi gave in and signed the final decree.

I wrote to Jack, expressing my sympathy to him about the miscarriage. I told him that my plans were set and that I was to be married that summer. Any hopes of my visiting the United States were probably over, or postponed. But in any case, if I came to America, it would be as a married lady, perhaps even as a young mother. But mostly, I wanted so much to let him know how important he had been to me, and I told him that.

I became Mrs. Anders Ekman on July 18, 1956, at a simple ceremony in my parents' apartment. The service went very well, except for one thing. I had been taking a nap just before the minister arrived, and when I got up, my hair looked very strange indeed, curled and damp. I quickly tried to fix it the best I could, but it just wasn't right. When I walked out to take my vows, Anders looked at me and said, "Good heavens, who did your hair?"

I was embarrassed. I said, "Oh, the hairdresser just around the corner."

Anders was angry. "Well, I'm going to find him and punch him in the nose for this!" he said. Fortunately, he forgot about it, and the poor hairdresser was spared.

But the wedding was lovely. In true von Post style, there were tasteful festivities arranged by my mother, and then we took off for Lapland, in the north, for fly-fishing and other pursuits, and I managed to survive it all. After a week of celebration, I started my new life as the *châtelaine* of Tjälls Gård.

In August, three years to the month after my first encounter with John F. Kennedy, my mother forwarded a letter sent to "Skyransgaten" (he never did get it right!), on U.S. Senate stationery, postmarked Hyannis-port, Massachusetts, and addressed to "Mrs. Anders Ekman" (absolutely correct). I tore it open, my heart beating with excitement. "Dearest Gunilla," he began. He said he was unhappy I was not coming to America, and sadder still that I was planning to marry "a farmer," but thanked God it wasn't that other "farmer," the one we had driven "halfway across Sweden to see last summer."

He then joked, tongue-in-cheek, that he and Torby were obviously irresistible to the opposite sex. Apparently Torby had flirted with one of the girls in Båstad and had been hoping to see her again when he and Jack—like the two jolly musketeers they were—visited again. But she had written Torby, saying that she, too, was getting married and that he was—under *no* circumstances—to return to Sweden!

Jack had been planning another visit, for the following summer. "To see *you*," he wrote, followed by a forlorn, "And now what will happen?" In spite of our last heartfelt, and I think for both of us, very painful, conversation, he still held out hope, and that same old powerful and romantic part of me did, too. Although I knew I could never betray a man as good and loving as Anders, my secret self thrilled at Jack's suggestion that if by some chance I *didn't* get married, I should come over and see him. But I felt a terrible conflict, too. It seemed as though Jacqueline's failed pregnancy was another blow against mending their union. Jack finished by telling me that I was a bright memory in his life, that I was *"wonderful"* and that he missed me.

I was very touched. I folded up his letter, slipped it

back into the envelope, and put it in my chest of drawers. I was wistful, but I had a home of my own now to attend to, and a good man to take care of.

Several weeks later, Ewa sent me a clipping. I had asked her to pick up the American papers from time to time for me. We got two Swedish papers up at Tjäll, and of course we had the radio and a black-and-white television set that brought in a few channels, though not terribly clearly. But my sister knew I would be interested in this: Jack had made a run for the nomination for vice president, but he had lost. The Democratic ticket was to be Adlai Stevenson for president and somebody named Estes Kefauver for vice president.

I hoped Jack wasn't too disappointed, but I remembered his saying he didn't think he'd make this one, anyway. He was definitely on a very important journey. I knew from my own history with him that he was determined to get his way, and I was fully prepared to believe that four years from now "the big job" might indeed be his at last.

～

Life at Tjäll was good from the beginning, although Anders and I had different styles of living. Because my heart muscle was not completely strong yet, I rested quite a bit during the day. I also liked to sleep late, while Anders was up at the crack of dawn. His early-to-bed-early-to-rise-and-off-to-the-hunt routine wasn't one I could share, but he was understanding. Besides, I had become a popular hostess, and I enjoyed entertaining and staying up late with our guests—usually the northern landowners and their families, the officers from the two neighboring regiments, and occasional visitors from Stockholm. Anders liked my spontaneity and sense of fun, and I never complained when he excused himself and went up to our bedroom for a good night's sleep while I stayed downstairs and tended to the party, often in our big kitchen.

More than anything, I wanted to start a family. Anders already had children by his first wife, and he loved being a father. Although my husband was a strong, caring, and ardent lover, I simply wasn't able to conceive, and after several months I began to worry it was because of my earlier struggles with typhoid fever. "Don't worry," Anders said to me. "I already have three children and I love you no matter what."

And then, I was genuinely happy to hear that Jacqueline had given birth to a beautiful, healthy baby girl, Caroline Bouvier Kennedy, in late November 1957. That gave me courage and hope. I realized that if I was meant to get pregnant, it wasn't necessarily going to happen on my schedule. We kept trying, and I kept praying.

~

To me, Anders was a reincarnated Marco Polo. Rigorous adventure seemed to fuel him. He loved taking risks and returning home triumphant, so I wasn't really surprised when, just after the beginning of 1958, he announced that we were going on a long, arduous, exciting trip.

"Where?" I asked pleasantly.

"We're sailing on a freighter/passenger ship from Gothenburg to El Salvador. Then we'll travel up through Mexico and across the United States to New York. We'll see so much—the ocean, the cities, the desert. Won't it be fun?"

"Oh yes, dear. But how will we travel through the desert?"

"We're taking the car."

I should have guessed. It was so like Anders to want to haul the big Mercedes 300 all over the world with him. And on top of that, I thought I might—finally—be pregnant. My doctor wasn't sure, but with my sometimes delicate health and tendency toward fatigue, he had recommended I take it easy. Just the right moment to career across oceans, mountains, and deserts for months.

But I could not, and would not, disappoint Anders. As a safety measure, however, I asked him if Ewa could come along. She was still unattached after her short marriage to Ernst Linder, and I knew she would enjoy the trip. Also, my sister was charming, very lively and most entertaining. She could keep Anders amused while I rested. He was delighted with the idea.

It was fun being three of only eight passengers with staterooms on the Johnson Line combined cargo ship. The voyage passed cheerfully enough, but the first day out, my suspicions that I had conceived strengthened. I took one bite of dinner and felt sick. I'm unconventional, so I had morning sickness at night. But the discomfort passed, and I was happy at the thought that I might be pregnant. For the rest of the journey, we ate with the captain each evening, and the food and wines were wonderful.

After clearing the locks of the Panama Canal, it was a short journey up the west coast of Central America. As we embarked at El Salvador, we watched aghast as one of the cables hoisting the Mercedes raveled and snapped, and the car went crashing down twenty feet onto the dock.

It took ten days to make repairs, so we stayed with some very wealthy, generous, and hospitable friends of my mother's, Dr. Beto Gomez-Mira and his wife, Lisa. I'd never seen such a contrast of great riches and abject poverty side by side as was on display in El Salvador. I said, "This place is ripe for revolution." They laughed at me.

At least the fighting didn't start while we were there, but quite enough thrills and spills were to come. If Anders craved adventure, he got plenty. The newly refurbished Mercedes was loaded on the flatbed of a freight train up through Mexico. Twice, while the train was waiting at whistle stops, bandits tried to untie and steal the car, but they were frightened away when Anders pulled out his pistol. I trembled at what this might be doing to my baby, but we pressed on. On a winding Mexican road we came upon a horrific accident between a car and a large bus. There was blood and broken glass everywhere. We stayed there for three to four hours, tending to the wounded. I was able to dispense painkillers and dress wounds. "You should get a medal," Ewa said to me.

It took seven weeks from the time we landed in Central America until we reached New York on April 9. Sometimes the highways were smooth and modern, but often we bounced and bumped over roads that were barely paved. Anders, who rose to the occasion of every wrong turn or traffic jam like a knight errant challenged by an adversary, was full of enthusiasm. As my pregnancy progressed, I became more and more tired. Ewa kept us all sane.

I had contacted Serge Obolensky again, asking if he would make arrangements for our New York stay. Since Serge was, *au fond,* one of those people who knew everyone everywhere, he could make life easier for them all, and upon our arrival in Manhattan, he did exactly that.

We were booked into a suite at the Ambassador Hotel, and when we arrived, Serge met us in the lobby. We must have been a sight. I know he was, but for different reasons. Wearing an expensive pin-striped, double-breasted suit with a white carnation in the lapel, he was a dapper, urbane sophisticate. We, on the other hand, must have looked like a trio of gypsies.

But Colonel Obolensky, the epitome of elegance, took no notice of our battered appearance and smoothly ushered us toward the bellboy, who put our bags on his trolley. Serge then asked us if we would join him for a pre-luncheon drink the following day, and glided off toward the exit, nodding greetings and shaking hands here and there like the great gentleman he was.

Anders finished registering at the front desk. As he turned to rejoin us, the reservations clerk called to him, "Mr. Ekman? There is a message here for you," and handed him a piece of paper.

Anders read it on our way up in the elevator. "Mr. and Mrs. Calder," he said.

"Who are they?"

"Some business friends. He travels quite a bit. I met him in Stockholm. Very nice people. I'm to call them."

I took little notice, as I was practically asleep on my feet. All I could think of was a bath and a bed.

~

I finished my bath, grateful for the warm soapy water that had soothed me after our long journey. I felt clean and comparatively invigorated for the first time in weeks, although the fatigue was still a dull undercurrent. I thought how nice it would be to curl up in the big hotel bed with crisply laundered sheets and fall off to sleep. I owed it to myself and to my new baby.

Ewa, fresh from her shower and wearing her favorite old terry-cloth robe, came into my bathroom.

"Where is Anders?" I asked.

"He's still on the telephone with those people who left the message."

"What people?"

"You know. Mr. and Mrs. Calder. Anders said they want us to go to some big benefit dinner dance tonight."

I sighed. "Well, this is one time I'm too tired for a party." I got out of the bath and Ewa handed me a large, thick towel with the Ambassador logo embroidered on it. After our dusty, bumpy journey, the pleasures of first class were absolutely wonderful. Wrapped up in the luxurious cotton towel, I dried myself gently and opened the bathroom door. I could hear Anders on the phone.

"Ya, normally we would be delighted. Well, we're all tired, and my wife is pregnant. So I don't think . . ." Then he laughed. "Oh, I'm sure the guest list is very impressive. Eric Rothschild? Ya, I met the baron once. Ya, Herve Alphand is the ambassador from France. The Kennedys? No, I haven't, but my wife met the senator once. I'm sorry, too, but—"

I pulled open the door and ran out to him. He was just about to say good-bye. "Anders, wait!"

"Just a minute." He put his hand over the phone.

"What Kennedys?" I said. "Where?"

My towel had nearly fallen off. "Cover yourself up, dear," Anders said, and helped to knot it around my waist. "Senator Kennedy and his wife. And a whole lot of others—other honored guests. It's the April in Paris Ball at the Waldorf-Astoria Hotel. I'm saying we can't go."

"Oh, but Anders, we must go! We just have to!"

"But my dear, you said you were so weary."

"Not anymore. When is it?"

"Eight o'clock, but—"

"I'll be ready!"

Anders continued on the phone: "Ignore what I

said. My wife and my sister-in-law and I will be happy to join you. Oh, you will? That's very kind. We'll be downstairs at ten to eight. Good-bye."

I looked through the few formal clothes I'd packed. "Ewa! Help me. This won't be easy." I pulled out something in off-white velvet and held it in front of me. "What do you think?"

"I can't tell. Put it on."

I slipped it over my head and tried to let it fall into place. Something was wrong. "It's tight," I said.

"You're pregnant," she said, already pulling out a black crepe de chine. "How about this? Black is slimming."

This one was tight, too. But better. Ewa gave me a quick once-over. "That's it." After finding a bright necklace and matching bracelets to go with it, I was ready. In deference to my black, Ewa put on a copper/gold sheath and looked as glamorous as always.

Shortly before eight, Lou and Lucille Calder were waiting for us in their car out in front, even though our destination was only a few blocks away. They were a pleasant couple with a great fondness for Anders. When we arrived at the Waldorf-Astoria, we made our way through the lobby and entered the Grand Ballroom. It had been transformed into a huge version of a French sidewalk café, with awnings and kiosks, and tables and chairs arranged around the dance floor. It was just a few minutes after eight o'clock. As we threaded our way through the room, moving closer and closer to the slightly raised dais at the front, I looked everywhere for Jack.

Suddenly, we found our spot. I was excited that the table was so close to the front of the ballroom. After we were all seated, I looked up again to see Jack and Jacqueline entering from the left together. He looked fit and had gained more weight, which was becoming. His wife, back in beautiful, slim shape after giving birth to Caroline in November, was coolly elegant. They sat at separate tables on the platform. Jack's was closest to ours.

I felt a secret thrill—secret, because Anders didn't know the extent of my friendship with Jack, although of course Ewa did. She gave me a knowing smile. I hoped Jack would spot me, but I was only one of many hundreds of faces there. The waiter was taking cocktail orders. When he got to me, I said, "Excuse me, but may I borrow your pen for a moment?" And he handed it to me.

I picked up one of the paper napkins that he had placed on the tablecloth for drinks, and I wrote on it, as clearly as I could:

SWEDISH GORILLA SITTING IN FRONT OF YOU!

I folded it in half and gave it to the waiter, along with his pen. "Would you please give this to Mr. Kennedy?" I asked.

"Just a moment, madam." He stepped aside and conferred with another waiter, a captain or maître d', and for a moment, I feared my message wouldn't get through. But the other man nodded, and then briskly walked up to the platform, strode toward Jack's chair, and leaned over. I saw Jack look up, smile, and take the napkin, which he unfolded and read in one movement. My heart was in my throat.

Jack stood up as though a bolt of electricity was coursing through him, and then he scanned the tables for only an instant and spotted me. His grin was incandescent. Still standing, he gestured with his thumb, poking vigorously at the air and pointing toward the hallway to his right, and started walking to the exit, glancing back and making it clear that I was to follow. I gathered up my purse and ran toward the corridor.

When I arrived outside in the hall, Jack stood alone, waiting for me. I wanted to rush into his arms, but this was a different place and time, and discretion ruled. Nevertheless, he embraced me quickly and kissed me on both cheeks. "It's marvelous to see you," he said, looking into my eyes. I don't know what emotions my face betrayed, but Jack's smile and expression and eyes registered everything.

"You look wonderful," he said.

"So do you."

At that very moment, I heard a scuffle of feet behind me, and at first I thought it was Anders and Ewa—I realized with some embarrassment that I'd simply abandoned them in my haste to meet Jack. But it was a photographer, an uninvited—and unwelcome—paparazzo. As I turned around, he yelled, "Mrs. Kennedy?" and a flash went off. In an instant, Jack reached for him, grabbed his camera, and smashed it onto the floor. The man picked up his broken camera and disappeared.

Suddenly, Anders and Ewa were there—probably thinking something was wrong, they *had* come after me. I quickly introduced Anders—he remembered Ewa from Båstad—but there was no time for conversation. Jack had his duty calling for him inside. "So very nice to meet you," he said to Anders, "but I'm afraid I have to get back."

"Of course," Anders said. He and Ewa began walking back to the ballroom.

For mere seconds, Jack and I were alone again. "It's great to see you," he said. He took my hand for the last time. I began to leave.

"Wait, Gorilla," he said.

His expression said everything I needed to know. In those wonderful, intense blue eyes I saw again the

Mediterranean Sea, and the stars above Båstad, and the bay below Sjöstugan where we swam. I felt the warmth of his body next to mine, and the tenderness of his kisses. I was flooded with the thrill of his embrace once more. If there is such a thing as time ceasing to exist, if an eternity can be experienced in less than a fraction of a second, then this was such a moment. But it all took place inside me. And the look on his face, as if he had gazed into my soul for that same instant, told me it was happening to him, too.

One memory, one mind, one heart.

He reached toward me and brushed the lock of hair from my forehead. No one saw us. He turned quickly and walked through the door into a room full of a thousand people.

I followed my husband and my sister back to our table.

~

My thoughts remained on Jack for the rest of that night and even into the next morning. Our midday cocktail with Serge led to lunch at "21," and the following day—the date of our departure from New York—I set out early to comb Manhattan's shops for baby clothes and toys, from Bonwit-Teller and Saks Fifth Avenue to Bloomingdale's and F.A.O. Schwarz. I was so distracted that I missed the embarkation of the *Stockholm* sailing back to Gothenburg that evening. To my horror, the gangplanks had been removed, and the ship was already under way, tugboats at work guiding the huge vessel into the harbor! I had to be taken out to board by a pilot boat.

At first Anders was furious with me, since he'd assumed I'd boarded much earlier. But I calmed him down, apologized, and said I loved him, because it was the truth. He was a wonderful man who cared for me deeply, and he was the father of the baby growing inside of me.

I left my bags and packages in our cabin and told Anders that I wanted to step outside, chilly as it was, for just a moment. I walked around aft of the ship and looked across the water churning below. Beyond the wide wake was the skyline of Manhattan. I wondered if Jack was still there. As New York faded into the distance, I knew I would return someday. I'd fallen in love with the U.S.A. There was the Statue of Liberty, so strong, dynamic, independent, and free. I said, softly into the wind, "See you again, America."

This time, I knew my last parting from Jack Kennedy had taken place—our third and our final good-bye. Jack had his life before him, his hopes, his ambitions, and his destiny. Maybe he would, one day, become president of the United States. If that's what he wanted, I prayed it would happen for him.

But I had begun another chapter. My future stretched before me, too.

I was going to be a good mother, and a good wife. I reminded myself that these were, after all, my lifelong dreams. I took one last look at New York before it was lost in the fog, and turned back toward our stateroom, pulling my big shawl around my shoulders and neck to ward off the damp and cold Atlantic air.

May 29, 1996

My Dear Jack,

This is a letter I have been longing to write to you ever since our last meeting in New York thirty-eight years ago. Of course, I couldn't have written it then, because we had no way of knowing what was to come. All we had was our brief past. And you were to have such a brief future.

I waited until this day to begin, because it is your birthday. You would have been seventy-nine. I wanted to feel close to you before starting, so I drove over to St. Edward's Church this morning and went in. You went there often when you were staying with your family in Palm Beach. As my eyes became accustomed to the cool, dark interior, I saw that it was filled with flowers! I don't really know the reason, because I'm not Catholic. But there they were, red and white carnations everywhere. And so many candles! I decided they were for you. I lit one "for absent friends."

I sat in one of the pews, and my thoughts grew profound. Perhaps I was praying, I don't know. But I was filled with your presence. And so many others'.

I grew to love Anders in a way I never dreamed possible. Yes, he was different from you as the fire of a volcano is from the salt of the earth, but he was protective, kind, and a wonderful father. After our return to Sweden, I gave birth to our first daughter. We named her Andrea. I regained my strength and even managed to accompany Anders and his comrades on hunting and fishing trips now and then. It wore me out, but I hung in, and thank God I like salmon!

It was a good life. Anders had always enjoyed piloting small aircraft, but his first wife, Mimmi, discouraged him from flying. I didn't. I thought it wasn't fair to deny him anything that gave him such pleasure; it would have been like saying, "You can't hunt. You can't fish. I won't let you ski." So he took it up again, and in 1960 we went to Munich to buy a new plane—a two-engine Dornier.

I wanted another baby, and although Anders said he'd had enough children from his first marriage, he said, "If you want more, I'm all for it. And I think it's a good time now." On our last night in Munich, I knew I had conceived.

We returned home to Tjäll and awaited delivery of the new Dornier. Meanwhile, Anders flew a borrowed plane.

I loved flying with him, belted into the cockpit by his side while he swooped and circled over the forests, rivers, and lakes of his domain. But there was a practical side to this sport, too; it afforded him a lookout for fires—important for a man overseeing thousands of trees.

Our cook, Kajsa, was a northern peasant with simple, old beliefs. She was wonderful and bright, and her superstitions were strong. At our dinner on March 29, 1960, Kajsa brought in the soup just as Anders was saying, "A peculiar thing happened today while I was skiing. I saw two black crows."

I thought I saw a strange look on Kajsa's face, but I said nothing.

Anders's plane was hangared at an airstrip thirty minutes from our house, called Kramfors. The next morning, because he planned to fly to Åre, a ski resort, we both arose early. But although I usually accompanied him, on this occasion I told him I preferred to stay at the house and care for little Andrea to give our nanny, Hilda, some time to herself.

Less than a half hour after he drove off, I heard a commotion downstairs. I went to investigate. Kajsa was running through the dining room, waving a broom. A huge wild cat, one we had never seen before, had somehow entered the house and was sitting on the dining room table. It rose on its haunches, and made hissing noises. She barely missed swiping it smartly with her weapon before the creature jumped down and disappeared.

I saw that same rather frightened expression on Kajsa's face as I had at dinner the night before, and I asked her what was going on.

"The strange animal in the house. The two crows Mr. Ekman saw. It's very bad."

"Bad?"

"It's a bad omen, Mrs. Ekman."

I was stunned, but I went back upstairs to Andrea, who was playing on our bedroom floor. Moments later, the sound of Anders's plane, flying low over the house, could be heard. I picked up Andrea and took her to the window. He was so close that I could see him through the windshield. I held up my baby's hand and we both waved as he disappeared over the woods, and I put her down to play again.

A few minutes later there was an odd noise, like a muffled crash, and then a sputtering crackle. As I started to run down the stairs, a little boy in a knitted red hat came running up. He screamed out, "The plane is on fire!"

I stopped for a moment, staring at him in shock. "But where is Mr. Ekman?"

"I saw something on four legs crawl out. I think it was him," the boy said.

I rushed out of the house, having thrown on a warm coat over my nightgown. I've never run so fast in my life. As I approached the flames, I kept screaming, "Where is Mr. Ekman?"

Our manager, Mr. Bolander, stopped me. "I'm sorry," he said, "but there isn't much left of Mr. Ekman."

My heart was racing. I felt as though I was having a nightmare. This couldn't be happening to me. How could anything destroy my strong husband, so full of life and vigor?

It was a freak accident, Jack. Along the edge of the grounds of Tjälls Gård flows the Angermanalven River, which the natives cross in the warmer months on a little ferry that is guided by a cable strung across the water between two pylons. Anders had ordered the cable removed for the winter, but it wasn't done. He couldn't see the wire against the snow, and his low-flying propellers got caught in the line, bringing the plane down.

Anders, a deeply caring father and a sincere, generous man, had left us. And now my whole world went to pieces. Back in our bedroom, I touched his pajamas and night robe, still warm. I felt lost and alone, grieving for my husband.

Twenty women who worked for Anders came to the house with flowers. Everyone was terribly kind. There was a huge funeral, and tributes from many of his friends, and the personnel of his company, Wäija Dynäs. I remained shattered for months, and I blamed myself because I hadn't insisted that he stop flying. But Anders wasn't completely gone from me. I was indeed pregnant again.

And then that summer of 1960, I went to London for a change of scenery. Our northern neighbors, the Kempe family, suggested I go to see an English psychic, Daisy Carter, while there. The Kempes told me she was a very famous and respected woman, not only a medium, but an opera singer and pianist as well. She had advised many world leaders, including Ernest Bevan, who was Britain's foreign minister, Labour Party leader, and one of the founders of NATO. Daisy Carter was legitimate. I made an appointment.

Daisy Carter was quite elderly by then. She welcomed me into her small but charming Maida Vale flat, and I sat before her. She looked at me for several minutes. She was kindly and serene. Then she said, "I see an explosion, a fire, some sort of accident. A car or something else is burning. A loved one is inside. It is your husband. He is no longer with us."

I explained. And I told her how guilty I felt.

"No, my dear. We have little to do with these things. On the day you are born it is decided when you are going to leave the planet. And when it is time for you to go, you go. Your husband might have just as easily fallen down the steps—who knows?" She looked at me again. "You are carrying his baby," she said with a smile.

Now I was truly touched and had tears in my eyes, because it wasn't showing at all, and I hadn't told anyone about my pregnancy yet.

She leaned toward me. "Gunilla, you are not alone. A love is coming. With someone of world importance. A king, or a head of state. But a very famous man."

"Maybe I already met him," I said, thinking of you, Jack.

"There's someone else. Remember, Gunilla, you have your whole life in front of you."

On December 22, Anders's second daughter, Rosina, was born.

I stayed in the north for two more years. Even though I had my children to care for, and the Tjäll staff, and the friends I'd made, the big house was lonely. So I moved back to Stockholm. I found a wonderful, spacious apartment on the grounds of Drottningholm Castle, in the cavaliers' quarters near the King's palace. It was extraordinarily beautiful, with hand-painted walls from the eighteenth-century, and I was very lucky to get the place.

They said you were warned not to go to Dallas, but you went anyway. On a wintry day in late November of 1963, both of my children were eating an early supper, and I took a moment to relax in my bedroom. My sister, Ewa, now a journalist, called and told me to turn on the television. The news was devastating.

At first I thought it was Jacqueline, but when I realized that you had been shot and killed, I turned off the set. I felt like an empty shell, as if my spirit, my entire soul, had just been snatched out of me. The vision of Anders's plane crash returned like a sudden nightmare. "Oh God, Jack, not you, too," I said to myself. And then I cried, for two lost loves.

But Jack, dearest, you died in your glory. Perhaps you would not have lived so much longer, anyway. Now the world knows what pain you endured all of your life, but I knew it, and felt it, while we were together. I think your courage was like a great curtain that you drew across yourself to hide your physical suffering. I have read much about your later dependency on the shots that Dr. Max Jacobson gave to you in New York in the early 1960s, and people have not been kind about that period. But maybe that doctor saved your life and kept you going as long as possible. I'm not writing this to judge, but to tell the truth.

Only a year ago, just around your birthday in 1995, you came to me in a dream. You knew about this book, and why I wanted to do it: to say that you were often misunderstood, and that your kindness and goodness changed my life. You said, "Tell our story and write what happened. Stick to the truth, and I'll be with you all the way."

Dear Jack, these are the thoughts that went rushing through my mind while I sat in that pew at St. Edward's Church this morning. I walked back out into the Florida sunlight. I drove past Green's drugstore, where you liked to buy ice cream. I turned around and drove toward your family's old mansion, now owned by someone else, but it will always remind me of you.

I have this place in Palm Beach because my second husband, Wisner Miller, was an American. He was a vice president of IBM and, like Anders, was considerably older than I. I was drawn to this man partly because of you, since I now loved everything American and wanted to live in the United States. But he was wedded more to his career than to me, and we parted. We had two sons. Wisner Miller III is now in his late twenties, living in New York, studying to be an actor. The other was dear little Ian, who died in my arms of leukemia after living only seven months. He had a great joy and zest for life. He just couldn't hold on to it very long. And his eyes were so blue and said so much.

As small as he was, he gave me great strength. When I buried him, I remembered reading many years earlier about the death of your own son. When Patrick Bouvier Kennedy was lowered into the ground, you touched his coffin and said softly, "Good-bye. It's awfully lonely down there."

I found Torby MacDonald again, and together we made a pilgrimage to the eternal flame in Arlington. Heavy with grief, he refused to get out of the car. As I approached your resting place, I was filled with admiration for Jacqueline and what she had done for you in life, and in death. I knelt down next to your grave, placed a single red rose there for you, and sent you all my love. When I returned to the car, Torby was unable to say a word.

A few years ago, I went back to Ruuthsbo. Gustav Hagemann, our "farmer" host, is still alive, and recently turned ninety. He calls the room you slept in "the Kennedy Room," and he has kept it exactly as it was when you and I were there. On my return visit, Gustav's son offered me that room.

That night, as I lay in bed, memories flooded back to me. I could not stop thinking of you and the love we shared. I felt joy for having known you, Jack, for having experienced what was truly inside your soul.

In the middle of the night, I was awakened by the sound of something falling. It seemed as though someone were in the room. I sat up. "Jack, what on earth are you doing here? Thank you for watching over me, and I will never forget you. Take care. I love you."

My parents have gone to where you are now. And Ewa, who died after injuries from an accident in Barbados. My second husband, too, and many others. I exchanged Christmas cards for a long time with Torby, and with Gavin Welby. Torby has left us, and Gavin's cards stopped coming years ago. I tried to find him in England, but I failed.

In your last letter, you wrote about what we had shared. You said it was one of your most vivid recollections. And you ended by saying, "You are *wonderful* and I miss you." Today, I can't say it any better than that.

Over forty years ago, you sent me a telegram from aboard ship while I waited for you in Sweden.

When the time comes for me to return to you, I'll whisper the same message up into the heavens. And you will hear me.

"*À bientôt.*"

Until then, my dear Jack,

Love always,

Gunilla

ACKNOWLEDGMENTS

I want to thank my three beloved children and my grandchildren: Andrea and Michael Sladek and their children, Janni and Eleonore; Rosina and Manuel Espirito Santo and their children, Eduardo, Isabel, and Ricardo; thank you H. Wisner Miller, Jr., for our son Wisner, who inspired me to write the book; to my nephew Nicolas; and Claudia Scier, who has also been of great help.

Many thanks to special dear friend Kirby Kooluris, who planted the seed in the ground.

Thanks to my cowriter Carl Johnes, and to my agents, Lane Zachary, Todd Schuster, and Esmond Harmsworth, who made the book possible.

I also want to thank Stan Winsten, who has taught me a lot about life in New York City. It is never too late to learn—"no bamboozling."

Warm greetings to the von Kantzow sisters, Lorle and Elfi, and their families. I want to thank my oldest Swedish friend, Anne Marie Glanzmann, for her encouragement and support, as well as my dear cousin Margaretha von Post in Stockholm. They both have given me good advice and helped me to brush the dust off old memories.

High up in Villars in Switzerland, my thoughts and thanks to old friends, to Jean-Louis Chable, who has been a great teacher in my life, and to Jacques and Jacqueline Bertinotti, as well as to my dear spiritual friend Felix Tercier.

And to my favorite dog, Igor, originally from Bordeaux, and to Dawa Ang, Sherpa from Nepal, who keeps praying for "Mamma Gunilla" to Buddha.

Thank you to all.
Gumilla von Post